Printed in China

中国四川新华印刷厂
Donated by

Tea and Tea Set

Appreciating Chinese Tea

Written by Li Hong
Translated by Zhu Jianting

CHINA INTERCONTINENTAL PRESS
WORLD CULTURE BOOKS

图书在版编目（CIP）数据

茶与茶具：英文/李洪著；朱建廷译.
-北京：五洲传播出版社，2009.12
ISBN 978-7-5085-1716-2

Ⅰ.①茶… Ⅱ.①李… ②朱… Ⅲ.①茶-文化-中国-英文 ②茶具-文化-中国-英文 Ⅳ.①TS971 ②TS972.23

中国版本图书馆CIP数据核字（2009）第199691号

Original Chinese language edition copyright © 2009 by China Light Industry Press

著　　者：李　洪
译　　者：朱建廷
选题编辑：荆孝敏 世界文化图书
责任编辑：王　莉 Lisa Zhang
装帧设计：宋索迪
设计制作：世界文化图书

出版发行：五洲传播出版社
地　　址：北京市海淀区北小马厂6号华天大厦
邮　　编：100038
网　　址：www.cicc.org.cn
电　　话：010-58891281
印　　刷：恒美印务（广州）有限公司
开　　本：889×1194mm　1／32
印　　张：5
版　　次：2010年1月第1版 2010年1月第1次印刷
07980（平）

Contents

Part 1 Knowing Tea from the Very Beginning

Part 2 Tea Set

Part 3 Tea and Tea Ware Q&A

Thanks to Jing Xiaomin, Li Mei, Madhumita Bardhan Sinha, Wang Li, Lisa Zhang and Suodi Song for their tireless efforts to make the project possible.

Select the Right Tea and Tea Set for a Perfect Cup of Tea

According to the famous writer Zhou Zuoren, "Tea ceremony, simply speaking, is snatching a moment of leisure from our busy schedules, seeking delight and experiencing its permanence for a moment in the harsh realities of life." These  words still hold good in the modern society today.

The beauty and harmony of the tea ceremony, the momentary permanence, brewing tea and sipping tea are enough to arouse eagerness in most people.

Brewing tea requires tea leaves, water and a tea set. Ancient people, closer to nature than the modern drinkers, brewed tea in rainwater, snow water, spring or well water. However, modern drinkers have many more choices in tea and tea sets in comparison with their ancestors.

Singling out tea and tea set from a number of varieties to brew a pot of the perfect tea and sipping it leisurely brings peace and happiness!

Shopping in a Supermarket

Tea

The tea supermarket, filled with tea fragrance, tea novelties, and interesting thumb-sized tea articles catch the customers' imagination.

China boasts innumerable tea varieties and develops more and more tea set patterns every day, easily making the customer feel lost in its wonderous varieties. Enjoy the ritual of choosing the right tea set. Stroll around the tea fragrance-permeated supermarket, have a cup of tea and talk with the vendor. Can you think of a more pleasurable experience?

Part I
Knowing Tea from the Very Beginning

Today, the number of tea drinkers in the world is on the rise. Iced black tea, iced green tea, chrysanthemum tea, Oolong tea and other tea-contained drinks are replacing carbonated ones and becoming the dominant health drinks in the 21st century. As the cradle of world tea plants, China enjoys affluent tea resources producing tea in 20 provinces (regions). Tea leaves are plucked from plants and processed into various tea through different technologies.

Do you remember how many kinds of tea you have tasted?

Tea-producing Areas in China

China was the first country in the world to discover, produce and consume tea some 4,000–5,000 years ago. Many scholars' studies on historical materials and Chinese wild tea plants prove Yunnan and southwestern China to be the cradle of global tree plants.

Tea-producing areas appeared in China as early as the Tang Dynasty (618–907). In his masterpiece the *Classic of Tea,* Chapter 8 Producing Areas, Lu Yu wrote about China's tea-producing areas in the Kaiyuan Period (713–741) of Tang as: 43 prefectures across 8 regions produced tea. The Song Dynasty (960–1279) witnessed the expansion of tea. During Yuan (1271–1368), Ming (1368–1644) and Qing (1644–1911) dynasties, tea-producing areas further expanded. The Opium Wars and other battles adversely affected tea production. Post the founding of the People's Republic of China (1949), China's tea production made new progresses, witnessing the recovery and expansion of tea-producing areas. Today, tea is produced in more than 1,000 counties and cities across 20 provinces, autonomous regions and municipalities.

▼ Tea-producing Areas of the Kaiyuan Period of Tang and Today

Period	Administrative divisions and tea-producing areas	8 tea-producing areas in the Tang Dynasty	
Kaiyuan Period of Tang	China consists of 15 regions: 43 prefectures across 8 eight regions produce tea.	Names of tea producing areas in Tang	Corresponding names of today
		Shannan Region, Huainan Region, Zhexi Region, Jiannan Region, Zhedong Region, Qianzhong Region, Jiangxi Region and Lingnan Region	14 provinces i.e., Sichuan, Hubei, Hunan, Jiangxi, Anhui, Jiangsu, Zhejiang, Fujian, Guangdong, Guangxi, Guizhou,Shaanxi, Henan (involving 241 counties and cities)
		Four tea regions today	
The People's Republic of China	20 of 34 provinces, autonomous regions, municipalities and SARs produce tea.	Southwest; south of Yangtze River; south China and north of Yangtze River across 20 provinces and autonomous regions, namely, Yunnan, Guizhou, Sichuan, Chongqing, Tibet, Shaanxi, Henan, Gansu, Shandong, Hubei, Hunan, Jiangxi, Zhejiang, Jiangsu, Anhui, Fujian, Guangdong, Guangxi, Hainan, Taiwan, involving 1,000+ counties and cities.	

Southwest Tea-producing Area

Southwest, including Yunnan, Guizhou, Chongqing, Sichuan, west Hunan, southwest Hubei, north Guangxi and southeast Tibet, is a plateau known for dark tea (including Pu-erh tea), green tea and black tea with a long tea-plant growing and tea-drinking history. It has abundant resources and varieties.

Famous tea

Pu-erh, Dianhong, Nanru and Baihao tea from Yunnan, Duyun Maojian, Zunyi Maofeng and Meijiang Cuipian from Guizhou, Mengding Ganlu, E'mei Zhuyeqing and Mengding Huangya from Sichuan, Tuocha from Chongqing, Jolmo Lungma holy tea from Tibet, Lingyun Yinhao from Guangxi, En'shi Yulu from Hubei and Guzhang Maojian from west Hunan.

North of Yangtze River Tea Area

In the extreme north, north of the Yangtze River, south of the Qinling Mountains and Huaihe River and east of the Yihe River, lies Shandong—appropriate for growing shrub middle- and small-leaf tea plants. This tea area, covering Shaanxi, Henan, north of Anhui, north of Jiangsu, south of Gangsu and Shandong, mainly produces green tea.

Famous tea

Wuzi Xianhao and Ciyang Maojian from Shaanxi, Xinyang Maojian from Henan, Lu'an Guapian and Shucheng Lanhua from Anhui, Bikou Long Jing from Gansu, Rizhao Xueqing from Shandong, etc.

South of Yangtze River Tea Area

South of the Yangtze River, boasting the longest history and most varieties of China's famous tea, is the most appropriate place for shrubs and small-sized arbor tea plants, producing green tea, black tea and Oolong tea, across Zhejiang, Hunan, Hubei, Jiangxi, south of Jiangsu, south of Anhui, north of Fujian and Shanghai and other areas in the south of the middle and lower reaches of the Yangtze River.

Famous tea

Long Jing tea and Anji White Tea from Zhejiang, Junshan Yinzhen and Gaoqiao Yinfeng from Hunan, E'nan Jianchun from Hubei, Lushan Yunwu and Wuyuan Mingmei from Jiangxi, Bi Luo Chun and Nanjing Yuhua tea from Jiangsu, Huangshan Maofeng and Taiping Houkui from Anhui, Wuyi Yancha, Zhengshan Lapsang black tea and Baihao Yinzhen from Fujian, etc.

South China Tea Area

South China tea area is one of the tea areas suitable for cultivating arbor or small-arbor tea plants mainly producing Oolong tea, black tea and green tea, across south of Fujian, Guangdong, Guangxi, Hainan, Taiwan and other areas in the south of Nanling Mountains.

Famous tea

Tie Guanyin and Huangjingui from Fujian, Yingde Black Tea and Phoenix Daffodil Tea from Guangdong, Liupu Tea from Guangxi, C.T.C. Black Fannings from Hainan, Dongding Oolong and Baihao Oolong from Taiwan.

Tea Classification Methods

Processing methods	Due to different technologies, the oxidation and quality of tea polyphenol are different. Thus, tea is classified into green tea, black tea, blue tea, yellow tea, white tea and black tea.
Production areas	20 provinces and autonomous regions produce tea in China: Zhejiang Tea, Fujian Tea, Yunnan Tea, Jiangxi Tea and Anhui Tea, etc. Pu-erh tea and Dianhong Gongfu Tea belong to Yunnan tea, Tie Guanyin, Huangjingui; Cinnamomum Cassia to Fujian tea.
Production seasons	Tea is classified into spring tea, summer tea, hot summer tea, autumn tea and winter tea. Spring tea plucked before Qingming is called Mingqian Tea, before Guyu called Yuqian Tea. Mingqian tea boasts the highest quality and price among green tea.
Quality grades	Quality grades are normally classified into Special, Grade 1, Grade 2, Grade 3, Grade 4 and Grade 5. Sometimes special grades are furthered as Special 1, Special 2 and Special 3. Pu-erh bulk tea has 11 grades. Grades are printed on the tea packing for easy identification.
Shapes	Tea shapes vary with tea varieties, such as needle tea like Anhua Pine Needle Tea, flat tea, such as Long Jing tea and Qiandao Jade Leaf, spiral tea, such as Bi Luo Chun and Mengding Ganlu, flake tea, such as Lu'an Guapian, orchid-shaped tea, such as Shucheng Lanhua and Taiping Houkui, single-bud tea, such as Mengding Huangya, straight strip tea, such as Nanjing Yuhua tea and Xinyang Maojian, bended strip tea, such as Wuyuan Mingmei and Jingshan Tea, and bead tea, such as Pingshui Bead Tea.
Distribution channels	Foreign sales tea, domestic sales tea, border sales tea and compatriots living abroad sales tea.
Processing degrees	Classified as primary tea, also called raw tea, refined tea, i.e., commodity tea and tea products and deep-pressing tea, i.e., instant black tea and tea polyphenol extracts, etc.
Fermentation degrees	Classified as non-fermentation tea, such as green tea, slight-fermentation tea, such as yellow tea and white tea, semi-fermentation tea, such as blue tea, full-fermentation tea, such as black tea and post-fermentation tea, such as Pu-erh tea.
Formation time	Historical tea, such as Guzhu Cisun and Xianshenzhang Tea; modern tea, such as Gaoqiao Yinfeng and Nanjing Yuhua Tea.

According to modern tea study, it is categorized as basic and processed tea, which is the most popular classification currently.

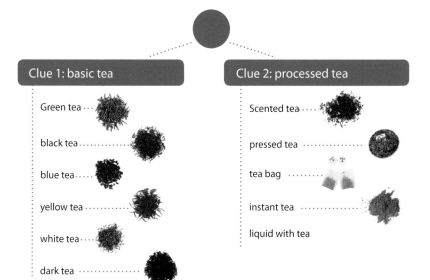

Clue 1: basic tea	non-fermentation tea	Green tea (Long Jing tea, Bi Luo Chun, Taiping Houkui, Huangshan Maofeng)	
	slight-fermentation tea	White tea (White Peony)	
	slight-fermentation tea	Yellow tea (Junshan Yinzhen)	
	medium-fermentation tea	Blue tea (Tie Guanyin, Dongding Oolong, Phoenix Single Cluster)	
	full-fermentation tea	Black tea (Dianhong, Qihong, Zhengshan Lapsang, Minhong)	
	post-fermentation tea	Dark tea (Pu-erh tea, Fuzhuan, Gongjian, Liupu Tea)	
Clue 2: processed tea			

Two Clues for Modern Tea Classification

Since ancient times, tea has been used as medicine, food and drink. Over the years, people's demands for tea has increased, and the tea process has also continuously changed. From eating fresh tea leaves to sun-drying for collection, from braising fresh green tea, tea cakes and fannings to green tea, black tea, blue tea (Oolong tea), yellow tea, dark tea, white tea and scented tea in Ming (1368–1644) and Qing(1644–1911) dynasties, the tea-processing technology has been constantly improved and upgraded.

At the end of the 20th century, tea liquids appeared in the market, along with various tea food and articles, witnessing wider and wider tea application.

Next, we'll study tea classification following the two clues of basic tea and pressed tea.

Green tea

Black tea

Blue tea

Yellow tea

White tea

Dark tea

Green Tea

TIPS

According to the *Classic of Tea*, tea application initiated from fresh tea-leaf chewing and then boiling for tea liquid. Later, people baked fresh leaves on fire and then boiled them, marking the earliest rough processing of green tea.

Modern production processes of green tea: plucking fresh leaves fixation (deactivating the enzyme in fresh leaves at high temperature, restricting the polyphenol enzyme in fresh leaves, promoting oxidation and preventing reddening) twisting and shaping drying. This is the rough processing of green tea also called raw tea.

● Lei Tea (ground tea), produced in Changde, Hunan, is also known as three-raw liquid. Its main ingredients are ground pastes of raw ginger, raw rice and raw tea (fresh tea leaves) and hot water. Today, Lei Tea is a local specialty and sometimes uses dry tea leaves in production. Dai and Wa ethnic groups still boil or brew fresh tea leaves for drinking. They often put baked fresh tea leaves into bamboo vessels or directly put fresh leaves into bamboo tubes to bake till softened and charred and then brew in water. This is known as bamboo tube fragrant tea. The tea liquid has a charred and sweet taste.

Four Main Technologies of Green Tea

Steamed green tea

Matcha tea powder

Exquisite steamed fixed green tea appeared in Sui (581–618) and Tang (618–907) dynasties. The *Classic of Tea* elaborated: "On fine days, plucking, steaming, smashing, beating, baking, penetrating and sealing the tea is done, and the tea is dried." This is the rough processing of green tea with steam for fixing, featuring green leaves, green liquid and green leaf leftovers. Japan-made green tea are mostly steamed fixed products, such as fried tea, Yulu and Tencha. In recent years, production lines in Zhejiang and Jiangxi provinces produce steamed fixed green tea, including tea bags and Matcha tea powder, mainly for export markets, such as Japan.

Roasted fixed green tea

Roasted fixed green tea boasts the highest output of all kinds of green tea in China. Tang Dynasty's poet Liu Yuxi wrote about it in his poem *Tea Tasting*, It is the earliest record on roasted fixed green tea, indicative of this process in the Tang Dynasty. Ming's first Emperor Zhu Yuanzhang issued a decree to "stop producing dragon dumplings and phoenix cakes, and pluck tea buds as tributes…" resulting in the popularity of bulk tea. The green tea processing technology also evolved from steamed fixation to roasted fixation, showcasing various famous

Long Jing tea

tea including Hangzhou Long Jing Tea and Anhui Guapian Tea.

Roasted fixed green tea deactivates the enzyme through roasting in pots in the rough processing and is dried through manual roasting in pots or a mechanical roaster or dryer in the drying process.

Different manual or mechanical forces result in various shapes of tea leaves classified as long, round and tender roasted fixed tea.

Roasted fixed green tea processed from tender fresh leaves has a unique and beautiful shape, jade green color, fresh and lingering fragrance, bright green soup and even essense leftover.

Baked fixed green tea

Baked fixed green tea requires charcoal fire or a dryer in the final drying process. Baked fixed green tea features complete buds and leaves, fluffy shape and knotted veins. Tender baked fixed green tea shows the fuzzy petiole in the clear, fresh and fragrant soup. The tea leaves are unbroken while the liquid is yellowish.

Liu'an Guapian

Sun-withered fixed green tea

Sun-withered fixed green tea refers to the green tea directly sun-dried during the rough processing. Drying in the sun is the most ancient tea-drying method used in Yunnan, Shaanxi and Sichuan—their tea products called Dianqing, Shanqing and Chuanqing, respectively. Sun-withered fixed green tea is seldom sold or consumed as commodity tea and is mostly compressed tea, including Pu-erh cake tea, Tuocha and Kangzhuan brick tea.

Yunnan ancient arbor sun-withered fixed green tea

It is characterized by the sun-dried flavor in the tea.

Today, new varieties of green tea processed through new technologies are constantly launched in the market. Some tea are dried through the combination of roasting and baking, such as Wuzi Xianhao of Shaanxi, Kaihua Longding of Zhejiang. This tea is unbroken and has the rich fragrance of roasted fixed green tea.

Green tea, as a kind of non-fermentation tea, normally uses tender leaves and follows the processes of fixing, twisting and drying. Bamboo-made tea baskets hold the plucked tea leaves. Detailed processes vary as do the shapes.

Currently, top-quality green tea are mostly manually processed, though some middle- and top-quality tea are mechanically or semi-mechanically processed.

TIPS

● Low caffeine-contained green tea can be made through hot water fixation technology since caffeine easily dissolves in hot water. After the dredging-up treatment, most caffeine in the fresh leaves dissolve. Thus, the caffeine content of the tea processed is low.

Mechanically processed Long Jing tea

Green Tea Brewing and Appreciation

Most green tea is made from tender leaves. The leaves are worthy of appreciation after absorption. Transparent glass without patterns is preferred for brewing to enjoy the dance of leaves. Apart from the visual enjoyment, porcelain cups are better for brewing green tea.

Brewing green tea, especially high-grade products, require strict water temperature range (75–85°). Low-temperature water will not activate the fragrance of green tea and too hot water will thicken and darken the soup, thereby "destroying the tea with heat." Normally, the proportion of tea to water is 1:50 for brewing in glass and flexible for different tea quality to cater to different tastes. Tea dipping methods are also important for green tea. Application of top-, middle- or bottom-dipping methods or different cups will have different tastes and fragrance for the same tea. Refer to the Tips on pages 36–49 for green tea brewing skills.

TIPS

● Water dispensers can heat water to 87°, allowing direct infusion of green tea. Water boiled in other heaters should be cooled to about 80°C before being used for brewing green tea.

Famous Green Tea

Long Jing Tea (Also Named Dragon Well Tea)

As the queen of green tea varieties, flat Long Jing tea is a typical roasted fixed green tea known for its "green color, strong fragrance, mellow flavor and good shape." Traditional Long Jing tea is completely manually roasted. Today, only top-quality Long Jing tea is manually roasted. Geographically, Long Jing tea is classified into West Lake, Qiantang and Yuezhou Long Jing. Long Jing tea is flat, with a straight smooth surface.

West Lake Long Jing

Tea liquid

Dry tea

Qiantang Long Jing

Tea liquid

Dry tea

Yuezhou Long Jing

Tea liquid

Dry tea

White Tea Long Jing

Dry tea

Tea liquid

[West Lake Long Jing is the best of Long Jing teas, while Shifeng Long Jing is the best of West Lake Long Jing teas.]

Shifeng Long Jing

Dry tea

Tea liquid

Bi Luo Chun

Bi Luo Chun was known as "Fearful Fragrance" and is a type of roasted fixed green tea. Emperor Kangxi of Qing Dynasty renamed it Bi Luo Chun. Originating from Dongting Hill (East Hill, West Hill) in Wuxian County, Suzhou, Jiangsu Province, it is also called Dongting Bi Luo Chun and noted for its "shape, gorgeous color, strong fragrance and mellow flavor." It has a spiral shape covered with white fuzz. With a strong natural fruit fragrance, it has a sweet and lingering taste.

TIPS

● Processing 500g top-quality Bi Luo Chun requires 60,000–70,000 tea buds.

● In areas producing Bi Luo Chun, tea plants and fruit trees are intercropped.

● Bi Luo Chun tea leaves are plucked early and sorted clean while they are still tender. Bi Luo Chun uses the top-brewing method with the water temperature at about 75°. (Refer to Tips on pages 38–40)

● Making balls is key in the Bi Luo Chun processing for the "compact spiral shape with fuzzy-white green leaves."

● Transparent glass without patterns is preferred for brewing Bi Luo Chun in order to view the dance of leaves. Porcelain cups though good do not permit this.

Xishan Bi Luo Chun

Tea liquid

Dry tea

Liyang Bi Luo Chun

[Dry tea is green with clear fragrance.]

Tea liquid

Dry tea

Fujian Bi Luo Chun

[Tea leaves are larger and with more white fuzz. Less fragrant].

Tea liquid

Dry tea

TIPS

● Currently, many provinces produce Bi Luo Chun, such as Jiangsu, Guizhou, Jiangxi, Sichuan and Fujian. The quality of products is similar to Dongting Bi Luo Chun in appearance. But the fragrance and flavor are quite different. Some counterfeit tea producers add chlorophyl and loquat fuzzes when processing Bi Luo Chun. Study the color and fragrance to identify authentic Bi Luo Chun.

Taiping Houkui

Orchid-shaped green tea Taiping Houkui, produced in Houkeng, Houcun and Hougang in Taiping County, Huangshan, Anhui, is baked fixed green tea. The leaves are straight; two leaves holding a bud within. Green with a natural orchid fragrance, its taste is fresh and sweet.

Manual Houkui

Dry tea

Tea liquid

Mechanically processed Houkui

Dry tea

Tea liquid

Liu'an Guapian

TIPS

- Lu'an Guapian is the rarely seen green leaf tea without a bud.
- Middle-brewing method in porcelain cups is preferred. (See pages 45–47 of *Brewing Tea* for pot infusion.)

Flaky green tea Liu'an Guapian is produced in Liu'an, Jinzhai and Huoshan of Anhui Province. Liu'an boasts high yield while Jinzhai boasts high quality. Neishan and Waishan indicates the production area. It is a single-leaf tea without stems and buds. A kind of baked fixed green tea, it has melon-seed-like dark green leaves with white fuzz on the surface. The green liquid has a lingering fruit fragrance, mellow flavor and sweet aftertaste.

High-quality Lu'an Guapian

Dry tea

Tea liquid

Common Lu'an Guapian

Dry tea

Tea liquid

31 •

Huangshan Maofeng

Orchid-shaped Huangshan Maofeng was originally produced in Taohua Peak, Ciyun Peak, Yungu Temple, Song'gu Temple and Ziguang Pavilion of Huangshan area, Anhui Province. Today, Xiuning, Qimen and Jixi are also produers. It is a type of baked fixed green tea. The golden Huangshan Maofeng is sparrow-tongued in appearance with white fuzz. It tastes fresh and sweet. Traditionally, the baking is over charcoal fire. In modern processing, Maofeng is mostly dried in drying machines.

Tea liquid

Dry tea

TIPS

● Huangshan Maofeng has ivory- and golden-colored leaves. Transparent glass without patterns is good to enjoy the dance of leaves. Middle-brewing method is used.

● During brewing, the leaves float on the surface at first and then start sinking or is suspended in the glass after absorbing water. The extended buds are pleasing to both the eyes and the mind.

Anji White Tea

Anji White Tea, a phoenix feather-like and bar-shaped green tea produced in Anji County, Zhejiang Province, is a type of semi-baked fixed green tea. In spring, new buds of the tea plant are light green, that change to white and back to green when leaves unfurl. The finished tea is puffy, light green in color, strong in fragrance and fresh in flavor.

Anji White Tea

Dry tea

Tea liquid
(Produced in other areas of Zhejiang)

Zhejiang White Tea

Dry tea

Tea liquid

E'mei Zhuyeqing

Flat green tea, E'mei Zhuyeqing, produced in Mount E'mei, Sichuan Province, is smooth and straight. Tender green buds float in the water at first and then stand erect at the bottom after absorbing water. The green liquid tastes fresh with a lingering aroma.

TIPS

● Transparent glass without patterns is best for brewing Zhuyeqing. The middle-brewing method is preferred. Enjoy the dance of leaves, breathe the fragrance and only then taste the liquid.

● Zhuyeqing is a new tea created in the 1960s named by Marshal Chen Yi.

Tea liquid

Dry tea

Ziyang Maojian

Bar-shaped green tea Ziyang Maojian, produced in Qinling Mountains, Ziyang County, Shaanxi Province, is curly, green in color, giving bright clear liquid and a sweet and longlasting fragrance. Ziyang Maojian has high selenium content.

Tea liquid

Dry tea

Kaihua Longding

Bar-shaped green tea Kaihua Longding, produced in Kaihua County, Zhejiang Province and also called Dalong tea, is compact and straight in appearance. The dry tea is jade green. The tea liquid is clear apricot green and tastes fresh and sweet with a lingering fragrance.

Tea liquid

Dry tea

Mengding Ganlu

Mengding Ganlu, produced in the Mengshan Mountain, Mingshan County, Sichuan Province, is a famous semi-baked fixed green tea with a curly and fuzzy appearance, light green color, light fragrance and fresh taste.

According to legend, the evolution of tea plants from wild growth to manual cultivation started from the Mengding Mountain. Wu Lizhen (Ganlu Period, Western Han Dynasty, 53 B.C.) grew seven tea plants. Wu was honored as Tea Ancestor and Master Ganlu.

Tea liquid

Dry tea

Xinyang Maojian

Bar-shaped green tea Xinyang Maojian, produced in Xinyang, Henan Province, is slender, straight with white fuzz. It is jade green and fresh in fragrance. It has a clear liquid and a sweet and mellow taste. The teas from Cheyun Shan, Tianyun Shan, Yunwu Shan, Jiyun Shan, Lianyun Shan, Heilong Pond and Bailong Pond are considered the best. It is from the northenmost tea-production area thus has the strongest flavor.

TIPS

● At the Xinyang Tea Festival Auction held in April 2006, a pack of 100g Xinyang Maojian named Lantian Yuye was sold for 149,000 yuan.

● The middle-brewing method is suitable for brewing Xinyang Maojian.

Tea liquid

Dry tea

Gaoqiao Yinfeng

Curved bar-shaped green tea Gaoqiao Yinfeng, a kind of baked fixed green tea produced in Gaoqiao Town, Changsha County, Hunan Province with the process created in 1959 by Hunan Tea Institute, is compact and curly and fully covered with silver fuzz, fresh and strong in fragrance, mellow in taste with bright and clear in liquid.

Dry tea

Tea liquid

Wuyuan Mingmei

Bar-shaped green tea Wuyuan Mingmei is produced in Wuyuan County called "the most beautiful village in China." Wuyuan lies at the border of Jiangxi and Anhui. In March 2005, the local government registered the trademark Wuyuan Green Tea. Wuyuan Mingmei is semi-baked and roasted green tea processed through fixing, twisting, baking, roasting and re-baking. It is slender and curly like eyebrows and covered with white fuzz. It tastes fresh and mellow with an orchid fragrance. The tea liquid is light green.

TIPS

● The middle-brewing method is used to brew Wuyuan Mingmei. When pouring water, the leaves look like flying plum blossoms. The 2nd brew has the best fragrance and taste which lingers after many brews.

● Wuyuan Green Tea has a strong fragrance, mellow taste, clear liquid and green leaves. In ancient times, most tea produced in Wuyuan were exported.

Tea liquid

Dry tea

Meitan Cuiya

Produced in Meitan County, Guizhou Province, it is flat, straight and smooth in appearance. The dry tea is yellowish-green. The tea liquid is bright green with fresh and longlasting fragrance and mellow flavor.

Dry tea

Tea liquid

Fried Tea

Produced in Japan, it is steamed fixed green tea with a compact shape, dark green in color, jade green liquid and a fresh taste. The brewed leaves are broken.

Dry tea

Tea liquid

Yellow Tea

Yellow tea was very popular in the Tang Dynasty. Ancient yellow tea were of two kinds: one made yellow during processing and one from the yellow leaves.

Processed yellow tea

The tea made yellow by processing is light fermented. Both the liquid and leaves are yellow. The production process is: fresh leaves → fixation → covering for yellow → drying. Yellow tea does not require any twisting after fixation. Some green tea show yellow liquid or leaves due to improper process or storage. They are deteriorated green tea. Yellow tea is classified into Huangya (yellow bud) tea, Huangxiao tea and Huangda tea according to the tenderness of the fresh leaves.

Famous Huangya tea

Huangyacha, i.e., Huangcha processed with strong buds, are further classified as Yinzhen (silver needle) and Huangya (yellow bud). The most famous Yinzhen is Junshan Yinzhen, produced in Junshan Island, Yueyang, Hunan. It is a rare yellow tea with a low yield. Huangya is classified as Mengding Huangya produced in Mengding, Mengshan Mountain, Mingshan County, Sichuan, Mogan Huangya produced in Mogan Mountain, Deqing County, Zhejiang and Huoshan Huangya produced in Huoshan County, Anhui.

Junshan Yinzhen

Produced in Junshan Island, Yueyang, Hunan, Junshan Yinzhen has strong and straight golden-colored buds covered with fuzz. The tea leaves stand erect in the water after brewing. The tea liquid is yellow and bright, with a fresh and strong fragrance. It tastes sweet and mellow.

Tea liquid

Dry tea

TIPS

● The brewed Junshan Yinzhen leaves look good.

Huoshan Huangya

Produced in Dabie Mountain, Huoshan County, Anhui, they looks like sparrow tongues. The buds and leaves are light yellow with tender fuzz. The liquid is bright green and fresh, the taste mellow and sweet. The brewed leaves are bright yellow and even.

Tea liquid

Dry tea

Mengding Huangya

Produced in Mengshan, Mingshan County, Sichuan, it is flat and yellow. The tea liquid is yellow and tastes sweet and mellow. The brewed leaves are light yellow and even.

Tea liquid

Dry tea

TIPS

● Huangxiaocha: Refers to the yellow tea processed with single buds having 1 or 2 leaves, such as Weishan Maojian, Beigang Maojian of Hunan and Luyuan tea of Yuan'an, Hubei.

● Huangdacha: Refers to the yellow tea processed with single buds having 3 to 5 leaves, such as Wanxi Huangdacha of Anhui, Dayeqing of Guangdong. The production is higher but the quality inferior to Huangxiaocha and Huangyacha.

● Yellow tea is hardly found in the market and finding an authentic one is even rarer. Due to various reasons, most yellow tea are made through the green tea process. Some yellow tea have totally disappeared from the tea world.

White Tea

White tea is special to Fujian Province having limited production. The production areas include Fuding, Zhenghe, Songxi, Jianyang. White tea has a history of more than 200 years.

Types of white tea according to process

White tea is lightly fermented. The preliminary process is: fresh leaves → sun withering → drying. It is classified as Baihao Yinzhen, Baimudan and Shoumei based on the tenderness of the buds. The white tea cools and detoxifies the body. It is mostly sold in Hong Kong, Macao, Malaysia, Singapore and other southeastern Asian countries.

Brewing white tea

The middle-brewing method is used for white tea. After pouring water, the tea will float on the surface at first and the buds will slowly straighten and settle at the bottom. Glass allows one to enjoy the dance of the tea leaves while porcelain cups will make it more fragrant.

Shoumei

Shoumei is produced from tea leaves. The bud is small and the leaves are naturally curled. It is gray and green. The veins are reddish. After brewing, the liquid is yellowish-green. The flavor is mellow and sweet and the fragrance fruity.

Tea liquid

Dry tea

Baihao Yinzhen

It is also called Yinzhen Baihao and made of fleshy buds. The tea is white and covered with white fuzz. In addition to the light fragrance and fresh taste, the tea liquid is a light yellow color and the brewed leaves are straight. Yinzhen produced in Fuding is called North Yinzhen and the one in Zhenghe is called South Yinzhen. There are two ways of making Baihao Yinzhen. One way is to peel followed by drying. Pick the tea leaves with one or two leaves in a bud. Keep the strong core leaves for making Yinzhen and use the rest for making Shoumei. The other way is to dry before peeling. Air the leaves till 80-90% dry. Peel away the other leaves and keep the core for baking dry over slow fire.

Tea liquid

Dry tea

Baimudan

Baimudan (White Peony) was first produced in Shuiji Town, Jianyang County in the early 19th century. Produced with tender buds, Baimudan has a fleshy appearance, joined buds and curly leaves. The gray leaves encircle the silver core, like a flower. After brewing, buds and leaves slowly unfurl, giving out a sweet and fresh fragrance. The apricot yellow liquid tastes like sweet potatoes and the brewed leaves are even and unbroken.

Tea liquid

Dry tea

TIPS

● The middle- or bottom-brewing method is used for brewing Baimudan. Refer to Tips on pages 126–130 for brewing skills.

Blue Tea

Blue tea, known as Oolong tea in the international market, has the fresh fragrance of green tea and the mellowness of black tea.

The earliest blue tea, Wuyi Yancha, appeared in the late Ming and early Qing dynasties. Later on, blue tea production spread to southern Fujian, Guangdong and Taiwan. In recent years, Wuyi Yancha is also produced in Hunan, Jiangxi and Sichuan, though the yield is low. Some Taiwanese tea merchants even introduced tea plants, advanced tea equipment and technologies suitable for processing Taiwanese blue tea. However, the quality is not satisfactory.

Blue tea processing

Blue tea is semi-fermented tea. The process involves plucking two or three fresh leaves → withering → partial drying → roasting fixation (fixation) → rolling and shaping → drying. Greening is a key process for blue tea quality. The unique greening, together with roasting fixation and shaping, result in the unique quality of blue tea. The process for blue tea varies according to regions and tea plant species.

Blue Tea Production Areas and Classification

According to areas of production— northern Fujian, southern Fujian, Guangdong and Taiwan blue tea.

According to appearances—bar-shaped (northern Fujian and Guangdong blue tea) and half-ball or granular (southern Fujian and Taiwan blue tea). Qualitywise—fresh and strong fragrance blue tea.

Northern Fujian Blue Tea

Northern Fujian blue tea is mainly produced in Mount Wuyi. It is also planted in Jian'ou, Jianyang, Nanping and Shuiji. Northern Fujian blue tea is the green tea well fermented. The tea processing starts from late April each year. Wuyi Yancha and Minbei Shuixian are famous products.

Southern Fujian Blue Tea

It is produced in Anxi, Yongchun, Nan'an, Pinghe, Hua'an counties.

Southern Fujian blue tea is normally lightly fermented. Tieguanyin, Huangjingui, Benshan Maoxie, Yongchun Foshou and Sezhong, etc. Tieguanyin boasts the highest quality and reputation.

Guangdong Blue Tea

Mainly produced in Phoenix Mountain Range, Raoping, and Meizhou. The species are Shuixian, Dancong and Sezhong. Phoenix Dancong and Lingtou Dancong are best in quality. Phoenix Mountain Range, with altitude above 1,000m, boasts excellent ecological environment.

Taiwan Blue Tea

Mount Ali, Nantou, Taizhong, Jiayi, Hualian, Gaoxiong and Taibei are the main production areas of blue tea. Taiwan blue tea, introduced from Fujian, is lightly fermented (Wenshan Baozhong and Dongding Oolong), moderately fermented (Muzha Tieguanyin) and well fermented (Baihao Oolong) tea.

Famous northern Fujian blue tea:

Wuyi Yancha

Wuyi Yancha is mostly named after the tea plants, for instances, blue tea made from Shuixian tea plant is called Wuyi Shuixian and made of Rougui called Wuyi Rougui. These are the dominant types of Mount Wuyi. Tea made from leaves of high-quality tea plants is called Dancong. High-quality Dancong is called Mingcong. Four Mingcong from northern Fujian blue tea were selected as the most Famous Bushes in the Guangxu Period of Qing Dynasty, namely, Dahongpao, Tieluohan, Shuijingui and Baijiguan.

TIPS

● Blue tea produced in Mount Wuyi is called Wuyi Yancha. The 60-sq.km.- region around Mount Wuyi, including 36 peaks and 99 rocks (yan), produce tea. Yancha is further classified into authentic Yancha, semi Yancha and Zhoucha. Authentic Yancha (best quality) refers to the blue tea produced in Huiyuanyan, Niulankeng and Dakengkou. Semi Yancha is also called small Yancha. Zhoucha's quality is inferior to semi Yancha.

Four Famous Mingcong:

Dahongpao [Big Red Gown]

Tea liquid

Dry tea

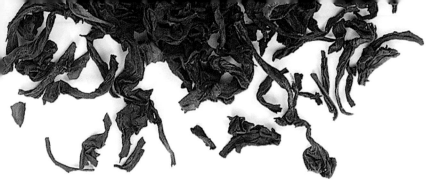

As the best of the Four Mingcong, the buds of Dahongpao are purple. From afar, the tree appears to be covered by a red gown. The six original Dahongpao tea plants, found in Jiulongke, Tianxinyan, have a 300-year-old history and an annual output of less than 1kg. At the 2005 Mount Wuyi Dahongpao Auction Meeting, 20g tea from the original Dahongpao trees were sold for 208,000 yuan. In 2006, Wuyishan Municipal Government announced Wuyishan Municipal Government's Decision on Special Protection and Management to the Original Dahongpao Tea Plants, to stop plucking the original Dahongpao tea plants, protecting the ecological surroundings and their survival.

In the 1980s, local tea institutes successfully cultivated Dahongpao tea plants. The processing of Dahongpao is with traditional technology and is more exquisite than other Wuyi Yancha. The leaves are even and compact. The color is fresh green. It has strong flowery fragrance and mellow flavor. The tea liquid is bright yellow. The brewed leaves are green with red edges. The fragrance still lingers even after seven or eight brewings. Currently, Dahongpao on the market are made from leaves of the asexually cultivated or transplanted tea plants and are called Xiaohongpao or 2nd generation Hongpao by tea merchants.

TIPS

● Be careful of tea merchants who sell other Wuyi Yancha under the name of Dahongpao.

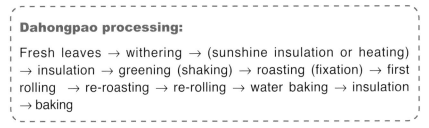

Dahongpao processing:

Fresh leaves → withering → (sunshine insulation or heating) → insulation → greening (shaking) → roasting (fixation) → first rolling → re-roasting → re-rolling → water baking → insulation → baking

Tieluohan (Iron Arhat)

Mingcong of Wuyi Yancha was originally produced in the Ghost Cave of Huiyuanyan, Mount Wuyi. Tieluohan tea plants grow in a narrow place between cliffs nourished by brooks. In recent years, a small quantity of Tieluohan tea plants are being cultivated and marketed.

It is said that this tea was discovered and made by an arhat (monk). Thus, it is named Tieluohan (Iron Arhat).

TIPS

● It has longlasdting fragrance and is a top-grade Wuyi Yancha.

Baijiguan (White Cockscomb)

It was originally produced in the Ghost Cave of Huoyan Peak, Huiyuan Yan. The matured leaves are dark green and lustrous. The tender leaves are thin, soft and white and are called Baijiguan (White cockscomb).

TIPS

● It is still fragrant after multiple brewings.

Shuijingui (Golden Water Turtle)

Originally grew in the Temple of Banyan under Dugezhai Peak of Tianxinyan. They were carried to Languyan of Niulankeng by flood. The precious tea tree appeared just like a golden turtle emerged from the water. The monks in the Leishi Temple named it Shuijingui. Because of the fight between the two temples, the tea plant is also called Guansicha (Lawsuit tea).

Dry tea

Tea liquid

Dry tea

Tea liquid

Dry tea

Tea liquid

Wuyi Rougui

It is made from the fresh leaves of the asexual Rougui tea plants. First discovered in Huiyuanyan, it has spread to the Sanlian Cave, Sanyang Peak, Matou Rock, Guilin Rock and Jiuqu Brook. The leaves are green, curly and compact with the fragrance of natural cassia barks. The main characteristic is its distinctive astringent taste. The brewed leaves are edged red and the liquid is mellow and yellow.

Dry tea

Tea liquid

Minbei Shuixian

Shuixian tea derives its name from the different technologies of processing—Minbei Shuixian if processed in Minbei blue technology and Minnan Shuixian in Minnan blue tea technology. Minnan Shuixian, introduced in Yongchun, southern

TIPS

● Crusted Minbei Shuixian has better quality, dense liquid and mellow flavor.

Fujian in the Daoguang Period of the Qing Dynasty, has thick veins, yellow color and a lingering orchid fragrance. The liquid is bright yellow, mellow and cool. It will be still fragrant after many brewings.

Shuixian Tea Cake

It is also called "tea in paper." Originally produced in Shuangyang Town, Zhangping, it later expanded to other areas of Zhangping. Fresh Shuixian tea leaves are plucked and compressed into a flat square cake tea with wooden molds. The process is that of Minbei Shuixian. The dry tea is black, and the liquid is dark brown and mellow. The brewed leaves are yellow and red-edged.

Dry tea

Shuixian

Shuixian, growing in the Zhuxiantao Cave of Jian'ou and Jianyang, was originally called Zhuxian. Zhu and Shui are phonetically the same and as the fragrance is like Shuixian (daffodil), it is called Shuixian. With its green and twisted veins Shuixian looks like a frog skin. The tea has an orchid fragrance, bright yellow liquid, mellow flavor and the brewed leaves are red-edged.

Dry tea

Tea liquid

Tieguanyin (Iron Goddess of Mercy)

Originally produced in Xiping Town, Anxi County, south of Fujian, it spread to Xianghua, Gande, Changkeng, Huqiu and Jiandou towns. In Anxi, tea plucking starts from middle April to continue through the year. Spring tea tastes good, autumn tea has great fragrance, followed by winter tea, and summer tea is the poorest in quality. Heavy, green Tieguanyin looks like twisted granules. Beautiful like Kuan-yin, heavy like iron, its liquid is golden, with a longlasting fragrance of orchids and a mellow flavor. The brewed leaves have silk-like luster and are fragrant even after seven brewings.

Tieguanyin rough processing: fresh leaves → sun withering → fixation → roasting for fixation → twisting → preliminary baking → packing twisting → drying. Fixation consists of alternately shaking and insulating 4–5 times and takes 8–10 hours.

Tieguanyin is a blue tea with the highest market share. As one of the most popular teas, Tieguanyin is expensive. It has great variety—dense fragrance, light fragrance, charcoal baked, ice fresh and preserved. Fresh Tieguanyin is best, so it is better to consume within the year of purchase. Some tea merchants mix other blue tea with Tieguanyin. Be careful when you buy tea!!

TIPS

- Ice fresh Tieguanyin, a special variety seldom seen in the market, should be kept in ice for freshness. The "dry tea" is compact and actually wet. Brewing needs more leaves than usual. It has a lovely fragrance and should not be brewed for long.

Dry tea

Tea liquid

Charcoal-baked Tieguanyin

Tea liquid

Dry tea

TIPS

● Charcoal-baked Tieguanyin is processed with modern technology. Mostly baked and dried in machines, charcoal-baked Tieguanyin uses charcoals to dry and bake the tea. It has a special fragrance and flavor and is seldom sold in the market.

Huangjingui
(Golden Osmanthus)

Originally produced in Anxi County and called "penetrating fragrance" by the locals, it is produced from the fresh leaves of the Huangdan tea plant. It is called the Golden Osmanthus. The leaves are plucked and sold earlier than other tea. The tea is curly and granulated. The taste is fresh. The brewed leaves are yellow and bright. The spring tea is the best.

Dry tea

Tea liquid

Benshan

Originally produced in Yaoyang, Xiping Town, Anxi County, the production has spread to Xiping, Huqiu, Changkeng and Weitian towns. It is one of the four major Anxi types and is dark green. The tea is granular and the taste fresh. The brewed leaves are yellow.

Dry tea

Tea liquid

TIPS

● Four major species of Anxi tea: Tieguanyin, Huangjingui, Benshan and Maoxie.

Maoxie
(Hairy Crab)

Dry tea

Originally produced in Fumei Village, Anxi County, it has spread to Daping, Huqiu, Penglai, Longmen and Lutian. Daping produces the best quality. The tea is dark green and granular. It tastes fresh and has faint flowery fragrance. The brewed leaves are thin and light.

Tea liquid

Baiya Qilan
(White Buds, Peculiar Orchid)

According to legend, there was a strange tea plant near a well in Pengxi Village, Qiling Town, in the Qing Dynasty. The buds were green with a little white. The tea had a special orchid fragrance, and was thus called Baiya Qilan (white buds, strange orchid). The dark green twisted and granular tea has a history of about 250 years. The fragrance is fresh and longlasting. The fresh and sweet tea liquid is bright and yellow.

Dry tea

Tea liquid

Yongchun Foshou
(Yongchun Citron)

TIPS

Also called Xiangyuan, Xueli, it is produced in Yongchun County, Fujian, and made from the fresh leaves of the Foshou tea plant. It was created in the Republic of China

● The leaves of the Foshou are oval and 2–3 timers larger than those of other tea plants.

(1911–1949). It is said a monk grafted tea spikes in citrons and processed tea from the leaves of the new tree. The tea has the flavor of citrons and is called citron tea. Later on, the tea spread to other counties.

Foshou, as a blue tea with a unique flavor, is twisted and granular. The leaves are thick and green with a lingering fragrance. The liquid is golden and bright. The brewed leaves are thick.

Tea liquid

Dry tea

Famous Blue Tea of Guangdong

Fenghuang Dancong

TIPS

● Fenghuang Shuixian, also called Shizhao tea, is one of the important Guangdong blue teas and made from fresh leaves of the Shuixian..

Guangdong blue tea is graded into Dancong, Langcai and Shuixian, of which Fenghuang Dancong is the best.

It was first created in the Ming Dynasty and produced in Fenghuang Town and Fenghuang Mountain. This tea was cultivated and reproduced from selected high-quality Fenghuang Shuixian. So, it was named Fenghuang Dancong. According to fragrance, it is classified into yellow branch, cinnamon, osmanthus, jasmine, orchid, almond, honey orchid, pomelo, yulan, yellow cape jasmine and everest types. The tea is of high quality, good shape, jade green color, dense fragrance and sweet taste. The liquid has a natural and lingering flowery fragrance and is bright and mellow. The brewed leaves are green with red edges. It can endure many brewings.

The tea brewed a day ago still smells sweet.

Tea liquid

Dry tea

Lingtou Dancong

Also called Baiye Dancong, it is produced in Lingtou Village, Pingxi Town, Raoping County, Guangdong. Lingtou Villagers Xu Muliu and Xu Jiashun discovered this special Dancong from Fenghuang Shuixian. The leaves are compact and curly. The color is brown. The liquid has a natural flowery fragrance. It tastes sweet and is bright yellow and endures brewing. The brewed leaves are red-edged green.

Tea liquid

Dry tea

Dongding Oolong

Dongding Oolong, produced in Mount Dongding of Phoenix Ranges, Lugu Town, Nantou County, is the best Taiwan blue tea. It is also planted in the nearby Fenghang and Yonglong villages. Farmers have to stiffen their toes (Dongding) to reach the peak of Mount Dongding, (700m high) to pluck the tea leaves. The half-ball curly leaves are green and oily. The liquid is bright yellow with a natural flowery fragrance. It tastes fresh and sweet. The brewed leaf is even and unbroken.

Tea liquid

Dry tea

Dongding Oolong rough-processing technology:

Fresh leave → solarization → drying in the air → rocking → roasted fixation → twisting → first baking → pack twisting (multiple) → re-baking → more baking

---

Wenshan Baozhong
(Wenshan Packed Tea)

Also called "clear tea," it is produced in Wenshan District, north of Taiwan. It is similar to the green tea in quality. The veins are curly and complex. It is dark green with a natural flowery fragrance. The flavor is elegant and light. The liquid is yellow. The brewed leaves are tender, even and unbroken.

TIPS

● Wenshan Baozhong originated from a packing method popular 150 years ago. Wang Yicheng, from Anxi, southern Fujian, imitated the Wuyi Yancha process method to produce Anxi tea and fumigated it with a flowery fragrance. The Anxi tea was packed into a 200-g square bag with a piece of Fujian paper citing the tea shop's name and address. The tea is popular and named Baozhong (packed) tea.

Tea liquid

Dry tea

Baihao Oolong

A deeply fermented blue tea mainly produced in Xinzhu County and also called Pengfeng Tea. The liquid is red and gives the tea the name Oriental Beauty. The tea leaves are covered with fuzz and are of five colors—red, yellow, white, green and brown. The flavor is mellow and sweet, and tastes fruity. The brewed leaves are unbroken and light brown with red edges.

Baihao Oolong has a funny origin. The tea is normally plucked in early June each year. In summers, a type of cicadas infest the tea plants. Tea farmers process this damaged tea plant with the blue tea technology. Surprisingly, it has a special flavor and is very popular. The tea was called Pengfeng Tea ("boasting" in the Kejia dialect) in the beginning.

Dry tea

Tea liquid

Black Tea

Black tea, created in the early 17th century (some believe that it was the 19th century), originated from today's Tongmuguang, Wuyishan City, Fujian. It is also called Souchong Black Tea, which is the first black tea in the world.

Types of black tea according to process

Black tea is characterized by red liquid and red leaves. The rough process technology of black tea is: plucking fresh leaves → sun withering → twisting or cutting → fermenting → drying. Black tea is classified into black strip tea and black broken tea. Black strip tea production requires full fermentation. The flavor is mellow and sweet. It is compressed by two rollers at different speeds, cut and rolled. The fermentation degree is light. The polyphenol content in the tea is high. The taste is strong and fresh. In general, red strip tea is suitable for drinking without seasonings while red broken tea is more suitable for drinking with other additives.

Red strip tea is classified into Kongfu and Souchong black tea.

Famous black tea: Souchong

Lapsang Souchong

It is classified into Lapsang souchong and Waishan souchong. Lapsang souchong, produced in Tongmuguan, Xingcun Village of Wuyishan National Nature Reserve, is also called Xingcun souchong or Tongmuguan souchong. Souchong, produced in Shaowu, Guangze, Zhenghe, Tanyang, Beiling, Gutian, Pingnan, Shaxian of Fujian and Qianshan of Jiangxi, is of poor quality and is called Waishan souchong or artificial souchong, no longer in the market today. However, thanks to its century-old popularity, Lapsang souchong is popular among European countries, especially the royalty of the UK. The leaves of the dry tea are compact and thick. It is dark with a lingering pine aroma. The liquid is yellow and tastes mellow with a longan flavor. The brewed leaves are thick and bronze-colored.

TIPS

● Black-processing pot: It is a special step to process souchong black tea to stop the tea fermentation. It preserves the tea polyphenol and reddens the liquid enriching its flavor.

● Souchong black tea has European and Chinese mainland flavors with different quality and features.

Tea liquid

Dry tea

The rough processing of souchong black tea:

Plucking fresh leaves → sun withering → twisting → fermentation → black-processing pot (fixation) → re-twisting → baking

Gongfu Hongcha
(Leisure Black Tea)

Souchong black tea appeared in China about a century earlier than Gongfu black tea. Gongfu black tea is a unique Chinese tea. The key for Gongfu black tea production is the time-consuming effort which is necessary for good tea. Gongfu black tea varies in quality due to the varieties of origins and tea plant species. The most famous ones are Qihong Gongfu from Anhui and Dianhong Gongfu from Yunnan. Others include Minhong Gongfu from Fujian, Ninghong Gongfu from Jiangxi, Yihong Gongfu from Hubei, Huhong (Xianghong) Gongfu from Hunan, Chuanhong Gongfu from Sichuan and Yuehong Gongfu from Zhejiang. It is classified into large- and small-leaf Gongfu according to tea plants.

Qihong Gongfu

Qihong Gongfu, also called Qimen Gongfu or Qihong in short, is produced in Qimen and its neighboring counties in Anhui. During the Guangxu Period in the Qing Dynasty, Qianxian-born Yu Ganchen planted a black tea plant similar to the Gongfu black tea. He planted another tea plant in Qimen to further expand black tea production. The geographical advantages give the processed black tea its natural aroma. Qihong Gongfu won the gold medal in the 1915 Panama Pacific International Exposition and topped export prices among all black tea. Lustrous black Qihong Gonfu tea has a strong honeyed sweetness. The liquid is red and tastes mellow. The brewed leaves are soft and bright. Qihong Gongfu is suitable for drinking without additives. When adding milk, the liquid turns pink.

Dry tea

Tea liquid

Dianhong Gongfu

Short for Dianhong, it belongs to the large-leaf Gongfu black tea and is mainly produced in Fengqing, boasting the highest quality (Lincang, Shuangjian and Menghai in Yunnan). The large-leaf tea plants are rich in polyphenol content. Theaflavins and thearubigins contents are high during processing. The quantity of lixiviated substances is also large after brewing. Dianhong Gongfu has compact leaves and smooth buds. It is brown and lustrous with golden fuzz. The high-quality products have more fuzz. The fragrance is fresh. The liquid is bright red with an outer golden ring. It has a strong and astringent taste. The brewed leaves are thick and bright.

High-quality Dianhong

Dry tea

Tea liquid

Common Dianhong

Dry tea

Tea liquid

Jiuqu Hongmei

Short for Jiuquhong, it is produced along the Qiantang River, Zhejiang. The leaves are compact and curly. It is lustrous black with even buds. The liquid is red, strong and mellow. Long Jing black tea produced in Hangzhou and Fuyang is actually Jiuqu Hongmei. The tea academy believes Jiuqu Hongmei, having a century-old production history, was originally produced in Jiuqu Brook, Wuyishan, Fujian. It is a kind of souchong Gongfu black tea. It is curly like hooks. The tea is lustrous black and tastes sweet and cool. The liquid is red and bright with quality parallel to Qihong Gongfu black tea. During the Taiping Heavenly Kingdom Period (1851–1864), the locals of Jiuqu Brook moved to the north of Zhejiang spreading the process of Jiuqu black tea to Zhejiang.

Tea liquid

Dry tea

Broken Black Tea

Broken black tea, also called graded black tea, is a dominant product in the international market and is about 80% of global tea export gross. In the 1870s, Indian George Reed invented the tea cutter to cut strip tea into broken pieces, marking the debut of broken black tea. The complete twisting and cutting during the production of broken black tea greatly destroy the leaf cells and lixiviate tea liquid, contributing to the oxidation and infusion of the polyphenol enzyme and the forming of its lingering fragrance, red and strong liquid and fresh taste. After adding milk and sugar, it is still strong. Ordinary broken black tea is more suitable for adding milk, sugar, honey, juice, coffee or other flavors. According to different twisting and cutting methods, it is classified into traditional, C.T.C., Rotorvane, L.T.P. and sun-withering-free broken black tea. They are further divided into leaf, broken, flake and powder tea based on leaf shapes. Quality and features vary greatly with the variety of production places and species. Broken black tea is mainly produced in Yunnan, Guangdong, Hainan, Guangxi, Guizhou, Hunan, Hubei, Jiangxi, Zhejiang and Jiangsu. The broken black tea processed from fresh leaves of the big-leaf species in Yunnan has the highest quality, while that from the small-leaf species is comparatively poor. Currently, most raw tea for home-made tea bags is from the broken black tea produced in Yunnan, Guangdong, Guangxi and Hainan.

Yingde Black Tea

Produced in the Yingde tea plant, Guangdong, it is a kind of broken black tea. The raw material used are mainly the big-leaf Yunan and some Fenghong Shuixian. Lustrous black tea with golden fuzz, with a strong and fresh fragrance, is highly popular in the international market. Red and bright liquid tastes mellow and is suitable for sipping with or without additives.

Black tea, as a kind of fully fermented tea helps resist cold and stimulate appetite.

Tea liquid

Dry tea

C.T.C. Broken Black Tea

It is granular and compact. Dry tea is lustrous black and brown. The fragrance is strong and the tea liquid is red with a strong, fresh and astringent flavor. The brewed leaves are red and even.

Tea liquid

Dry tea

Brewed leaves

Mixed tea liquid

Dark Tea

Dark tea is a necessity for the ethnic groups living in Tibet, Xinjiang, Inner Mongolia and northwestern regions where tea is more important than food. Dark tea is mainly produced in Yunnan, Sichuan, Hunan, Hubei and Guangxi.

As early as in the Northern Song Dynasty (960–1127), rough green tea leaves were processed to dark tea. Dark tea's process is: fresh leaf plucking→fixation→twisting→pile fermentation→drying. For easier transportation, tea leaves are compressed, such as Fu brick tea, dark brick tea, Kang brick tea, Green black tea, Jinjian tea, Liubao tea, Fangbao tea, Qizi cake tea and Tuocha tea. Traditional black tea, normally dark brown, uses coarse and old tea as raw material and tastes temperate.

Hunan Dark Tea

Hubei Dark Tea

Hubei dark tea mainly refers to the blue brick tea produced in Yangloudong areas.

Blue brick tea engraved with "China" in Chinese characters

Blue brick tea with Chinese character "Chuan."

Guangxi Dark Tea

It refers to Liubao tea produced in Liubao Township, Cangwu County. The tea is dark brown with luster. Dark reddish-brown, the tea liquid tastes sweet and strong, the flavor is of betel palm and it has a lasting aftertaste. Liubao Tea features red color, strong taste. The tea with the golden "fungoid flowers" is the best.

Liubao Tea

Tea liquid

Dry tea

Hunan Dark Tea

Hunan dark tea can be classified into Xiangjian Tea, Fuzhuan Tea, Heizhuan tea and Huazhuan tea. Fuzhuan Tea has a "fungoid flower" with a unique fungoid flavor.

Fuzhuan Tea

Cross-section of Fuzhuan Tea

Qianliang Tea

Tea liquid

Section of Qianliang Tea

Fuzhuan Tea

Dry tea

Tea liquid

Gongjian (Tribute Shoot Tea)

Dry tea

Tea liquid

Tianjian

Dry tea

Tea liquid

Sichuan Dark Tea

Sichuan dark tea can be divided into Nanlubian Tea and Xilubian Tea, including Kangzhuan Brick Tea, Gloden Shoot Tea and Fangbao, etc.

Kangzhuan Tea (Brick Tea)

Dry tea

Tibetan tea of China

Jinjian (Golden Shoot Tea)

Dry tea

Tea liquid

TIPS

● As the dark tea is completely fermented and mostly compressed, the tea leaves are broken.

Yunnan Dark Tea

Yunnan dark tea mainly refers to Pu-erh tea, which is made from Dianqing loose tea with the pile fermentation process and normally compressed into Qizi tea cake, brick tea or Tuocha, etc.

Qizi tea cake

Pu-erh Tea

The history of Pu-erh tea can be traced back to the East Han Dynasty, originally produced in Xishuangbanna and Simao area, Yunnan province. Pu-erh tea produced from the six famous tea mountains (Mansa, Yiwu,Manzhuan, Yibang, Gedeng and Youle) are the most famous. Pu-erh tea is created from the green Maocha broad-leaf tea variety and compressed into different specifications. The tea was discovered in Puer and thus named Pu-erh tea. After hundreds of years of changes and development, Pu-erh has reached its current popularity today. The tea picking season is from late February to November, but the tea picked in the spring is the best.

Pu-erh tea raw cake   Pu-erh tea ripened cake

Pu-erh tea has more than one tea types, but normally is classified into raw tea and ripened tea according to the processing technique.

Raw Pu-erh tea

Green Maocha made from the large-leaf variety, is in either loose form or compressed form of different shapes.

Processing technique:

Green large tea leaves→fixation→twisting→drying→Dianqing Green Maocha→natural fermentation→loose tea
└→compressed into shape→cake tea

Pu-erh tea Shaiqing (sun-baked) Maocha

Dry tea

Tea liquid

Pu-erh tea silver shoot tea cake

Dry tea

Tea liquid

Ripened Pu-erh Tea

The raw tea stored and fermented naturally can be stored for more than 15 years. Pu-erh tea, after fermentation according to the traditional process, becomes milder. In the 1970s, the artificial pile fermentation technique was introduced, enabling Pu-erh tea reach the desired quality in a short time. This kind of Pu-erh is called ripened tea, i.e. Pu-erh with artificial fermentation, or Pu-erh with modern processing. This kind of ripened tea, after being stored for a time, sometimes several months, can be distributed in the market. The high-quality ripened tea is maroon or dark maroon. The liquid is dark red, clear and tastes mellow, smooth and sweet, without any musty odor.

Processing technique:

Green large-leaf tea leaves→fixation→twisting→drying→ classification→pile fermentation in moisture→airing→ picking→ripened loose tea
 ↳pressing and drying→compressed into shape→ripened tea cake

Ripened Pu-erh loose tea

Nv'er Cha (Maiden tea)

Dry tea

Tea liquid

Pu-erh Tea in Different Shapes

Golden melon tea

Ornamental Pu-erh tea

Mini tea cake

Tuocha

Pu-erh brick tea

Mini Tuocha

Appreciate the ripened tea, enjoy the result. To enjoy the aging flavor of Pu-erh tea, you will have to choose the high-quality ripened Pu-erh, which is red and clear, with minor changes in color and flavor after multiple brewings. It has a strong aging flavor without foreign odors.

Raw Pu-erh tea must be preserved for a long time, normally more than ten years or even longer. But the result is worthy of the expectation.

Clue 2: Processed Tea

The processed tea refers to the reprocessed or refined product made from the raw tea of the six basic kinds of tea. According to the processing method and approach, the processed tea can be classified into scented tea, pressed tea, tea bag, instant tea and tea beverage.

Scented tea

Tea bag

Molded scented tea

Pressed tea

Instant tea

Tea polyphenols tablets

Scented Tea

Scented tea, also known as the fumigated tea, or fragrant flower tea. The basic tea is fumigated with flowers to extract its essence. Scented tea is mainly produced in Fujian, Guangxi, Yunnan, Sichuan and Zhejiang provinces.

History has recorded the adding of camphol to tea as early as the early Song Dynasty. Though it cannot be considered as genuine scented tea, adding flavor to the tea could be considered the nascent stage of the scented tea. Fumigating tea with jasmine originated from the Song Dynasty. There were records of fumigating tea with orange peel or lotus in the Ming Dynasty. During the rein of Emperor Xianfeng of the Qing Dynasty, scented tea was mass produced.

Fumigated Tea

Fumigated tea has always been a favorite drink of the Chinese, especially those in north China who favored jasmine tea in particular. The quality of the fumigated tea is subject to the quality of the basic tea, flower and the fumigation process. The fumigation process of jasmine tea is complex: first process the jasmine and the basic tea, then mix the fresh jasmine (blooming in the evening) with the tea and keep the mixture aside for fumigation; after the first fumigation, sieve the flower and dry the tea; and then fumigate the tea with the fresh jasmine for a second time, the third time…. High-quality fumigated tea normally undergoes three to five fumigations. The fumigated tea is packed directly without drying along with a small quantity of high-quality fresh flower. This process is called *tihua* (enhancing flavor). The lower-quality fumigated tea is normally fumigated only once or twice, or with used flowers.

The fumigated tea is named after the flower it used, for instance, jasmine tea, white michelia tea, Zhulan tea, Daidai tea, sweet-scented osmanthus tea and rose tea. The jasmine tea is the best in quality and largest in quantity. The basic tea used is mostly the baked green tea, black tea or blue tea.

Jasmine Yinzhen Tea

The best basic tea is the Yinzhen tea produced in Fujian. It is needle-shaped with silvery fuzz and has a fresh and strong flavor. The brewed leaves are even.

Tea liquid

Dry tea

Jasmine Longzhu Tea

The ball-shaped fuzzy Jasmine Longzhu Tea is strong with the Longzhu flavor overshadowing that of the Yinzhen tea.

Tea liquid

Dry tea

Bitan Piaoxue

Bitan Piaoxue produced in Sichuan is the best from a tender basic tea, compact and curved in shape and a small quantity of dry jasmine. This kind of tea, yellowish-green, has a lasting flavor and the brewed leaves are tender and even.

Tea liquid

Dry tea

Maiden Ring Jasmine Tea

Rolled in the shape of a ring, the tea leaves unwind to display the whole shoot when brewed.

Tea liquid

Dry tea

Jinsui

In the shape of wheat ear, Jinsui tea unwinds when brewed to display the whole shoot.

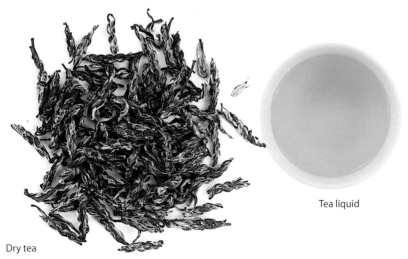

Tea liquid

Dry tea

Rose Black Tea

With the fragrance of rose, the tea is of a glossy dark color and has a sweet taste.

Tea liquid

Dry tea

Sweet Osmanthus Black Tea

The sweet osmanthus black tea is made from the C.T.C. fannings tea. The osmanthus flowers are not picked out. The dried flowers are in the ready black tea.

Dry tea

Molded Scented Tea

The molded scented tea is different from the fumigated tea. Dry flowers and tea leaves are mixed and molded into various shapes for ornamental purposes. The flavor and taste is inferior to the fumigated tea.

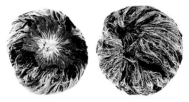

Molded scented tea

Pressed Tea

The pressed tea, or compacted tea, is made from bulk tea after being pressed into different shapes. It can be divided into pressed green tea, such as the bamboo tube tea produced in Yunnan; pressed black tea, e.g., Mizhuan tea produced in Hubei; pressed blue tea, e.g., Narcissus Tea Cake produced in Fujian; and pressed dark tea, which is the largest in quantity, such as the Qianliang tea produced in Hunan and Pu-erh tea produced in Yunnan.

Tea Bag

Tea bags can be divided into the single bag and double-bag variety if classified according to appearance. Classified by the tea in the bag, it can be divided into the green tea bag, black tea bag, blue tea bag and healthy tea. They are convenient to carry and easy to brew.

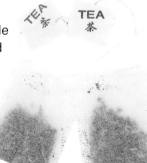

Instant Tea

Instant tea, also known as extracted tea was first produced in China in the 1970s. Instant tea is made from the concentrated soluble tea substances dried into grain or powder. Instant tea leaves no dregs and can be made with cool water too. The flavor and the taste are not as good as that of tea leaves. There are instant black tea, instant green tea and instant jasmine tea, etc.

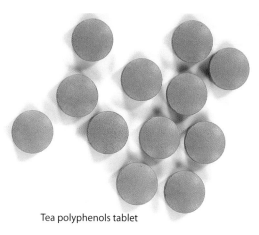
Tea polyphenols tablet

Instant Tea Powder

Tea powder

Tea liquid

Tea-flavored drinks

Tea-flavored drinks refer to the liquid containing tea substances, such as the black tea liquid, green tea liquid and Oolong tea liquid, in addition to the tea wine and tea milk.

Tea Substitute

The root, stem, leaf, flower, fruit and peel of some plants can be brewed or boiled with water, drunk separately or with others. Though they do not belong to the category of tea, they are called tea. In China, we call them tea substitute.

Flower and grass tea

Herbal tea

Fruit tea

Grain tea

Flower and Grass Tea

In the western countries, flower tea is as popular as basic tea in China. Flower tea is easy to get and make, without caffeine but with the fragrance of a flower or plant. It can help you relax. It has become a trendy health drink.

There are many flowers and grass that can be made into tea, such as the chrysanthemum, rose, sweet-scented osmanthus, jasmine, lavender, mint, roselle, honeysuckle, purple perilla, mulberry leaves and the lotus leaves. Both the fresh leaves or flowers, and the dried flowers or leaves can be made into drinks if brewed in hot water, or boiled, or with ice cube, and can be drunk separately, or together with the other flower, grass or fruit or herbal drinks.

Sweet Osmanthus Tea

Sweet osmanthus, or Dangui, Yingui, Sijigui and Yangui in Chinese, has a strong fragrance and can be used to brew wine, or eaten or made into scent bags. It tastes pungent and can be used to treat asthmas, ease rheumatism, joint pain and stomachache, etc.

Tea liquid

Dry tea

TIPS

● Gargling with the sweet osmanthus tea can cure halitosis.

Sweet osmanthus icy tea

Preparation: 3–5g dry osmanthus, sugar or honey and ice cube
Brewing: In a cup or pot, put the osmanthus into the container and add boiled water, keep for 3–5 minutes and then add sugar or honey, and the ice cube.

Sweet osmanthus milk tea

Preparation: 3g dry sweet osmanthus, sugar, and milk, 3g C.T.C. black tea fannings
Brewing: Make the sweet osmanthus tea, and then add the sugar and milk.

Sweet osmanthus milk tea liquid

Mint

Mint, also known as mint leaf, tastes cool and refreshing. It can help alleviate headache, cure cold, stop itching, detoxify and remove halitosis. Together with tea, it tastes better.

TIPS

● Mint has a strong flavor and must be sealed tightly, otherwise its fragrance will affect other products.

Mint tea

Preparation: 2–3g dry mint leaves, honey or sugar
Brewing: Put the mint leaves into the container and add boiling water. Keep for 3 minutes before drinking.

Dry tea

Tea liquid

Chrysanthemum

Chrysanthemum has a history of more than 2,000 years in China and can be divided into Gongju, Hangbaiju, white chrysanthemum and yellow chrysanthemum. It is mainly produced in Anhui and Zhejiang and the neighboring areas. The chrysanthemum, slightly cool in property, can reduce body heat, detoxify, detumescence, is diuretic, nourishes liver, eyesight, lowers blood pressure and soothes nerves. In addition to making liquid, it can be used to make conjee or dishes. What's more, using pillows made with the dry chrysanthemum can help cure insomnia.

TIPS

● Yellow chrysanthemum, tastes a little bitter, is more effective in fever-clearing and detoxifying; the white chrysanthemum tastes sweet and is more effective for the liver and improving eyesight.

Gongju

Hangbaiju

Wild chrysanthemum

Golden chrysanthemum

Chrysanthemum Pu-erh Tea

Preparation: Pu-erh tea (ripened tea), 3–5 pieces of chrysanthemum
Brewing: Add boiling water to the Pu-erh tea and chrysanthemum in a small
pot. Or put the chrysanthemum directly into a cup and add the Pu-erh tea
liquid. Enjoy the elegant aging flavor of the chrysanthemum.

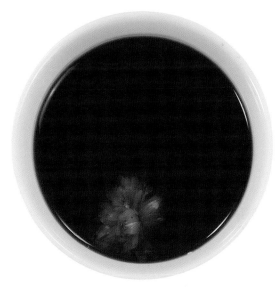

Chrysanthemum Pu-erh tea liquid

TIPS

● Chrysanthemum conjee

Prepare chrysanthemum and rice. Moisturize the dry and odor-free chrysanthemum
with boiling water and add to the rice in a pan. Alternatively, stew the chrysanthemum
in boiling water for about 3 minutes, and then take out the chrysanthemum. Put the
rice into the syrup and make the conjee according to normal methods.

Chrysanthemum conjee is soothing and nourishes eyes. In the hot summer, add ice
cubes in the conjee to get icy chrysanthemum conjee.

Rose Tea

Rose, also called *feihong* in Chinese, has a strong fragrance. It is mild and tastes a little bitter. It helps blood circulation, tones the blood, relieves menstrual discomfort and makes the skin radiant.

Roselle

Roselle, also called *luoshenhua* in Chinese, has an acid flavor. It can help cool the blood and relieve the summer heat. It helps blood circulation, removes halitosis and clears the skin. Take 2–3 petals of roselle and pour boiling water, keep for about 3 minutes and add sugar or honey before drinking.

Tea liquid

Dry tea

TIPS

● Those who have weak spleen and stomach should avoid roselle syrup.

Herbal Tea

Herbal tea is made from herbal medicines to help to cure diseases. Some compound herbal tea may contain animal organs or minerals. Today, herbal tea is widely used as remedies—the cooling herbal tea, weight-losing tea, stomach-strengthening tea and the blood pressuring-lowering tea. Herbal tea is made into tea bags and canned tea drinks, easy to carry and drink.

You must be prudent while choosing herbal tea. Consult a doctor as soon as any discomfort arises. The common herbal tea materials include medlar, cinnamon, Juemingzi, licorice, Sterculia lychnophora, Motherwort, Ginkgo biloba, American ginseng and ginger slice.

Dry ginger

Licorice

Dwarf lilyturf

Medlar tea

The medlar tastes sweet, has mild properties, and is a traditional Chinese medicine. It helps nourish the blood, fortify the kidney, stimulate the appetite and enhance immunity. It can be used for making wine or dishes.

Medlar tea

5–8g medlar, brew in a cup or pot with boiling water.

Medlar

Medlar tea liquid

Ginseng tea

American ginseng

Tea liquid

Juemingzi tea

Juemingzi looks like the mung bean and so is named the fake mung bean. It is slightly cold, tastes sweet with a tinge of bitterness. It can help strengthen the stomach, reduce greasiness, smooth the intestines and alleviate chronic constipation.

TIPS

● Some flowers or plants are also herbal medicines and often used in compound herbal teas.

Juemingzi tea

6–8g Juemingzi, brew in a cup or pot with boiling water. It also can be boiled to make a drink or be drunk together with the chrysanthemum or sweet osmanthus.

Juemingzi

Tea liquid

Sterculia lychnophora

Sterculia lychnophora inflates after absorbing water. It tastes sweet and is beneficial for the throat, cough and lung. Sterculia lychnophora is often used together with liquorice to make a drink.

Sterculia lychnophora tea

1–2 pieces of sterculia lychnophora, 1–2 pieces of liquorice. Brew in a cup or pot with boiling water. Drink after 3–5minutes.

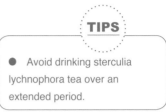

TIPS

● Avoid drinking sterculia lychnophora tea over an extended period.

Tea liquid

Sterculia lychnophora

Fruit Tea

Fresh fruit or dry fruit can be made into a drink after being boiled separately or together. Made with fresh fruit or dry and refined natural fruit, the fruit tea has a sweet flavor with the slightly acidic and strong fragrance of the fruit and flower. It can be made with boiled water or ice cube. This kind of tea strengthens the digestive functions. It is better to drink after a meal.

There are all kinds of fruit teas of different quality and origin, such as the Flavor of Europe, Blue Danube, Swimming Beauty and Elegant Girl. It is recommended to select the dry fruit tea with natural and fresh flavor. The liquid of the high-quality fruit tea must have a good transparency. The fruit tea should be stored in the refrigerator after sealing tightly.

Tea liquid

Dried fruit

You can make the fruit tea yourself.

Prepare fresh fruit, such as a pear or apple or dry fruit, such as the Chinese date, longan, medlar and chrysanthemum and a black tea bag. Wash the fresh fruit and dice them, and wash the Chinese date, longan, medlar and chrysanthemum. Add the raw materials into a glass pot or stainless steel pot of boiling water and boil for 3–5 minutes on slow fire. Add the black tea bag and brew for 3 minutes. You can enjoy the liquid and eat the raw material.

Grain Tea

The grain not only can be eaten, but also be drunk.

Mung Bean Tea

The mung bean has cooling properties. It helps detoxify the body and relieve the summer heat. It is often used for making conjee or cake, and also as a hot or cold drink.

Mung bean

Tea liquid

Buckwheat Tea

The buckwheat tea has cold properties and is bitter in taste, but rich in rutoside. It can help improve the microcirculation, lower the blood sugar and the blood pressure, and improve the immunity of the human body. It can be brewed in boiling water or boiled. The boiled buckwheat is edible.

Buckwheat

Tea liquid

Part 2

Tea Sets

In the past when tea was used as food or medicine, there was no concept of a tea set. But when tea became popular as a drink the need for a tea set gradually emerged. In more than 1,000 years, the tea set evolved with the development of tea drinking. With increasing precision and perfection, it finally became an important part of the Chinese tea culture.

Different Meanings of Tea Set in Ancient Times

Origin of tea set

The origin of the tea set cannot be separated from the discovery and utilization of tea. In different periods, the tea set played different roles. There was no special tea set when tea was used as food or medicine. It was separated from the other ware when tea became a drink in the daily life. The tea set originated from wine ware or cookware. In the western Jin Dynasty, Zuo Si's poem *Beloved Daughters* had such sentences "eager to have a cup of tea, blow and heat Ding (cooking vessel) quickly." Ding could have been the earliest tea utensil.

With more cultural relics unearthed in recent years, the archaeologists believe the emergence of the tea set latest by time of the Han Dynasty.

Ancient tea set and modern tea set

With gaining popularity, the ancient tea set ,gradually transformed into a complete category. The earliest recorded tea set was in Lu Yu's *Classic of Tea*. In Volume 2 Tea Tools and Volume 4 Tea Ware, Lu Yu records in detail the tools used for picking tea and ware used for brewing tea. In the Tang Dynasty, the 15 tools used for picking and making tea were named "tea tools" and the 28 utensils used for boiling and drinking tea were named "tea ware."

Imitation Jianyao Kiln Tianmu Cup

These titles were used till the north Song Dynasty. With evolving tea drinking methods, these were renamed "tea set" in the south Song Dynasty and the name is still used today.

The modern tea set evolved from the ancient tea set according to the types of tea and tea-making methods. It mainly refers to the utensils used for brewing and drinking tea, including the water boiler, tea-making device, tea appreciating appliance and auxiliary appliances. Trendy and easy to use, the modern tea set meets the requirements of different types of tea and different brewing methods.

Modern Tea Set

People in the olden times highly valued the tools of making tea. Tea sets of the different periods had their own distinctive styles. Today, new tea sets can be seen in the market every day showcasing different designs, colors, raw materials and refined functions to cater to the modern tea-making styles.

Modern tea set are of pottery, porcelain, glass, bamboo, wood, calabash, metal, jade and various composite materials.

Pottery

Pottery was an important Neolithic invention. Made from clay burned in kilns at 700–800°C, it is hard in texture, with or without a glazed surface.
The common tea sets include the purple-clay pottery (also called boccaro) and hard pottery.

Ceramic tea set

Ceramic tureen and Gongdao cup
(Fairness cup)

Ceramic teacup

Purple-clay Tea Set

The purple-clay tea set is produced in Dingshu Township, Yixing, Jiangsu Province. The purple-clay is high in iron and silicon content, featuring high plasticity. The tea set made from the purple-clay is not normally glazed (except Wenxiang cup and Pinming cup). The finished product is primarily purple, thus it is named the purple-clay cup. This

Red purple-clay pot

Purple-clay pot

Tree Burl Pot

TIPS

● Mansheng Pot

The famous Qing Dynasty Mansheng Pot was not made by Chen Mansheng. Chen Hongshou, also called Mansheng, of Qiantang, Zhejiang (Mansheng) loved the purple-clay products and worked out 18 designs. Mansheng Pot normally had the Chinese lettering "Amantuo Shi" and "Made by Chen Mansheng" on the bottom and the seal of "Pengnian" on the handle. Those pots were mostly made by Yang Pengnian, Yang Fengnian and Yang Baonian based on Chen's designs. Only a few Mansheng Pots have survived and are a collectors dream.

pottery can be divided into different colors, such as the purple-brown pottery made from the "purple clay" which is in amaranth or light purple; the gray-yellow product made from the "green clay" in gray or gray-blue; and the vermeil product made from the "red clay" in red-brown.

The purple-clay pottery tea set has a long history in China. It is believed that Su Shi, great scholar of the Song Dynasty, designed a pot with a handle. In his memory, the pot was named "Dongpo Pot with Loop Handle."

In the Ming Dynasty, making loose tea in a small pot was popular, which led to the development of the purple-clay pot.

Gong Chun was the first potter who chiseled his name "Gong Chun" on the Shuying Hu (Tree Burl Pot). Following his lead were Dong Han, Zhao Liang, Yuan Chang, Shi Peng, Shi Dabin, Li Zhongfang, Xu Youquan, Hui Mengchen, Chen Mingyuan, Yang Pengnian and Shao Daheng during the Ming and Qing dynasties.

Purple-clay with Loop Handle

Clay used for making the purple-clay pot

Today there are many famous potters in Yixing with their own unique styles. The purple-clay tea set may or may not be inscribed or painted. It includes the purple-clay cup, tea tray, Gongdao cup, Pinming cup, Wenxiang cup, coaster, pot holder and lid holder, etc.

Purple-clay tea set

Porcelain

Porcelain is one of the greatest inventions of ancient China. In the late East Han Dynasty, the Chinese mastered the porcelain burning technique and ancient China was named the "Porcelain Country." The porcelain is fired in kilns at temperatures above 1200°C. The porcelain tea set has varied types, designs and colors.

Three-piece bone china tea set

Blue-and-white porcelain tea set with ball patterns (set)

Blue-and-white porcelain tea set with flower patterns

The porcelain tea set can be divided into the white porcelain, celadon, blue-and-white porcelain, painted porcelain and color-glazed porcelain.

White porcelain

The body is pure white, translucent and smooth. It is mainly produced in Jingdezhen, Jiangxi Province, Dehua, Fujian Province, Chaozhou, Guangdong Province, Liling, Hunan Province and Tangshan, Hebei Province.

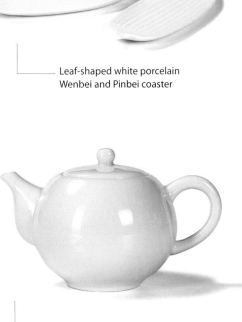

Leaf-shaped white porcelain Wenbei and Pinbei coaster

The white porcelain and blue-and-white porcelain tea sets are the most popular. The teapot, teacup, tureen, Gongdao cup and coaster have the largest varieties, designs and colors. The white porcelain tea set can set off the true color and taste of the tea and display its natural beauty.

White porcelain teapot

Travel tea set made of white porcelain

Celadon

The celadon is famous for its exquisite texture, smooth lines, beautiful shape and glazed layer. Zhejiang Longquan celadon is the most famous. In the Song Dynasty, the celadon fired by brothers Zhang Shengyi and Zhang Sheng'er's Geyao Kiln and Diyao Kiln reached a high artistic standard. Today, new breakthroughs have been made to improve the traditional celadon process of Longquan. The types include celadon thin base, underglazed color celadon, the combination of celadon and white porcelain. The celadon tea set is valuable as it is rare and is very popular in Japan and Korea. Making tea in the celadon tea set sets off the clear green color of the green tea liquid.

Mini celadon cup

Celadon tea set

Celadon teacup

Celadon tea set (cracked surface effect)

Black porcelain

"To set off the white tea liquid, the black porcelain tea set is the best." The black porcelain tea set was praised highly during the period of the Song Dynasty, especially Heizhan (black cup) produced in Jianyao, Fujian. Jianyao Kiln Heizhan, also called Tianmuzhan, had a thick highly glazed porcelain body. After firing, the porcelain could display many different designs, like hair, oil drops or partridge. The tea liquid adds to the glazed luster.

Black porcelain teacup

Color glaze

The color-glazed porcelain is the tea set of today. There are various kinds, such as the red glaze, green glaze, yellow glaze, blue glaze, purple glaze, tea fannings colored glaze and so on.

Color-glazed appreciation cup

Painted color-glazed teapot

Color-glazed appreciation cup

Painted porcelain

The technique combining painting and porcelain firing first started in the Tang and Song dynasties and became popular in the Ming and Qing dynasties. There are blue-and-white, Doucai (contrasting color), Tiancai, enamel and other color patterns; different symbols denote different meanings.

Colored landscape porcelain pot

Doucai tureen

Aroma cup and appreciation cup with chrysanthemum painting

Covered bowl with blue pattern

Appreciation cups

Glassware

The glass tea set started late in China, but developed quickly. Glass can be divided into the common glass, tempered glass, crystal glass and synthetic glass. The glass tea set normally is colorless with high transparency and high temperature resistant performance. It is perfect for brewing the tender shoot tea, such as the high-quality green tea, yellow tea and white tea, good for appreciating the tea. The drawback of the glass tea set is its quick conductivity and fragility. Normally the glass cups have thick bases. The common glass tea set includes the teacup, Gongdao cup, Pinming cup, tureen and water boiler.

Glass tea set

Glass teacup

Glass tea set

Tea Ware Made of Bamboo, Wood and Calabash

The tea ware made of bamboo, wood and calabash has a long history in China. For instance, mention of "clipper, gourd ladle, basket and sieve" is found in Lu Yu's *Classic of Tea*. The raw materials of the tea ware are cheap, easy to get and simple to make. The common tea ware include tea tray, tea tools, coaster, tea holder and tea screen, mostly used as the auxiliary tools for brewing tea. Some minorities widely use bamboo cup, wood bowl and gourd paddle in everday life. Tea ware made of rare raw materials having exquisite workmanship is normally expensive and can be collected for its artistic value.

Bamboo and wood strainer

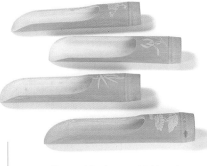

Chaze with plum, orchid, bamboo and chrysanthemum patterns

Gourd strainer

Double-layered tea tray

Metal Tea Ware

Metal tea ware can be of gold, silver, copper, tin and stainless steel. Metal tea ware are corrosion resistant. In ancient times, gold and silver tea ware symbolized affluence. A large quantity of gold and silver tea ware were unearthed in 1987 in the underground palace of Famensi, Fufeng county, Shaanxi.

Stainless steel instant kettle

Tin tea canister

These included tea grinds, Chaze and tea powder cases, etc. Today, metal tea ware is commonly used and includes airtight tin tea canister of different shapes and copper water kettles for boiling water. Cloisonné enamel tea ware first started during the Jingtai period of the Ming Dynasty. Mostly tureen and teapot, the cloisonné enamel tea ware is exquisite, luxurious and elegant. Stainless steel tea ware includes the water boiler, tea strainer and disinfection pot. These tools are bright and clean and airtight, and are good conductors of heat. Normally equipped with manual and auto control functions, they make great traveling cups, but are not good for brewing tea.

Other Tea Ware

Plastic cups, paper cups, enamel cups and stone cups are used in everyday life. But these are not good for brewing tea. There are also jade or stone tea ware with exquisite carving. Such tea ware are more popular as collectibles than practical use.

Jade tea holder

Zipao Yudai stone tea tray

Zipao Yudai stone tea tray

Tea Ware List

Tea ware classified according to functions include the water boiler, primary tea brewing ware and auxiliary tea brewing ware. Classified according to form they are the single tea ware and the combined tea ware.

Single Tea Ware

Water Boiler

The common water boiler is the electric kettle— safe, convenient, pollution-free and fast. The power is normally 400W to 1800W (higher voltage will boil the water faster but power consumption will be more). High-temperature resistant glass pot and pottery kettles often use ethanol as fuel (pottery kettles use charcoal). These kettles are slow to boil and unsafe, which you can use when boiling water in the open country.

Pottery kettle and oven

Ethanol oven and glass water boiler

Electric kettle

Electric instant water boiler

Teapot

The teapot, normally small in size, is used to brew tea. There are porcelain teapots, purple-clay teapots and glass teapots each best for brewing tea of different kinds.

Porcelain teapot

Purple-clay teapot

Ceramic teapot

Glass teapot

Covered bowl (Gaiwan)

The covered bowl, also known as the Sancai bei and Chazhan, is often used as a substitute teapot in south Fujian. It also can be used as a teacup. It is normally used for brewing scented tea. The covered bowl is normally porcelain.

Pink-colored covered bowl without saucer

Glass covered bowl

Blue porcelain covered bowl

Purple-clay covered bowl

Porcelain covered bowl with Duicai

Pottery covered bowl with spout but without saucer

Color-painted "Longevity" covered bowl

Doucai covered bowl

Fencai covered bowl

Teacup

The teacup normally refers to the cup with large capacity, best for everyday tea brewing. Teacups may be of glass, porcelain, purple-clay and ceramic. Brewing in a teacup is convenient, but not good for tea appreciation. Normally the tools used for appreciating tea are small—150–200ml is the best.

Three-piece purple-clay tea set

Painted white porcelain teacup

Teacup with green glazed landscape

Mini blue porcelain cup

Handmade ceramic teacup

Handmade ceramic teacup

Hand-painted white porcelain teacup with saucer

Big bone porcelain teacup

Color-painted pottery teacup

Purple-clay teacup

Painted white porcelain teacup

Purple-clay teacup

Glass cup

Gongdao Bei (Fairness Cup)

The Gongdao cup, also called the Chazhong or Chahai, is used for holding and mixing the tea liquid.

When brewing tea, the liquid is poured into the Gongdao cup to prevent the liquid getting stronger or bitter from over brewing. The Gongdao cup, first used in the 1970s, was larger than the matching pot or covered bowl. The common Gongdao cup is of porcelain, purple-clay and glass, with or without handle. Some Gongdao cups have a strainer.

Blue-and-white Gongdao cup

Gongdao cup with chrysanthemum Duicai

Red-glazed Gongdao cup

Painted yellow-glazed Gongdao cup

Colored Gongdao cup with pine and crane painting

Purple-clay Gongdao cup

Ceramic Gongdao cup

Purple-clay Gongdao cup

Purple-clay Gongdao cup

Glass Gongdao cup

Glass Gongdao cup

Appreciation Cup (Pinming Bei) and Aroma Cup (Wenxiang Bei)

Also called Wen and Pin cups. Appreciation cup, the size of a half Ping-Pong ball, is of different shapes, such as a half ball, single-layered or double-layered. Most aroma cups are made of porcelain and few are purple-clay cups with white glazed interior.

TIPS

● In a tea ware set, some may not have a matching aroma cup, only an appreciation cup.

Glazed appreciation cup

Blue-and-white glazed appreciation cup

Blue-and-white appreciation cup with landscape painting

Glass appreciation cup

Glazed ceramic appreciation cup

White glazed purple-clay appreciation cup

Blue-and-white porcelain appreciation cup

Painted Fushou (luck and longevity) aroma cup and appreciation cup

Hand painted appreciation and aroma cups

Green glazed aroma and appreciation cups with tray

Hand painted landscape aroma and appreciation cups on a wooden tray

White-glazed purple-clay aroma cup

Ceramic appreciation cup

Purple-clay appreciation cup

Glazed ceramic appreciation cup

Glazed ceramic appreciation cup

Blue porcelain appreciation cup

The aforementioned tea ware are used for brewing tea. The following auxiliary tools are also necessary.

Tea Tray (*Cha Pan*)

The tea tray, also known as the Chachuan (tea ship) and Chaxi (tea wash), is used for carrying the tea brewing tools and the waste water. There are single-layered tea trays and double-layered tea trays. In a double-layered tea tray, the first layer has holes while the lower layer is a drawer for draining water. The single-layered tea tray only has a metal pipe in the right lower corner to drain the waste water into a connected waste tea bucket. The tea tray is normally made of bamboo or wood, and sometimes ceramic, purple-clay, stone and jade.

TIPS

● The double-layered tea tray has limited capacity to hold the waste water and should be cleaned timely to avoid overflow.

Double-layered bamboo tea trays (the right bottom one with an electric instant water boiler)

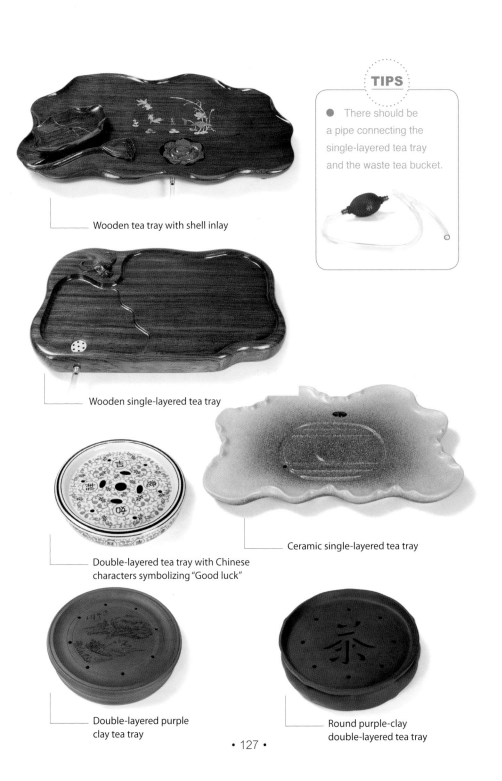

Wooden tea tray with shell inlay

TIPS

● There should be a pipe connecting the single-layered tea tray and the waste tea bucket.

Wooden single-layered tea tray

Ceramic single-layered tea tray

Double-layered tea tray with Chinese characters symbolizing "Good luck"

Double-layered purple clay tea tray

Round purple-clay double-layered tea tray

Waste Bucket
(*Fei Cha Tong*)

The bucket holding the waste water and tea dregs is the waste bucket. Different from the common trash bin, it is normally made of bamboo, wood, plastic or metal. The sieved first layer has an opening connected to a pipe.

TIPS

● The tea dregs can be stored in the second layer of the double-layered tea tray.

Plastic double-layered waste bucket

Wood and bamboo double-layered waste bucket

Stainless steel double-layered waste bucket

Strainer and Srainer Holder (*Lvwang and Lvwang Jia*)

The strainer, also known as the tea filter, is used for filtering the tea residue. It should be placed on the holder when not in use. It is made of the stainless steel, ceramic, calabash, wood or bamboo.

Plastic strainer and holder

Metal strainer

Ceramic strainer and holder

Metal strainer and ceramic holder

Ceramic strainer holder

Metal strainer and ceramic holder

Metal strainer and holder

Calabash strainer and ceramic holder

Tea Holder (*Cha He*)

The tea holder is a container used for storing the dry tea temporally for appreciation in tea ceremonies. Most tea holders are made of porcelain.

Porcelain tea holder

Porcelain tea holder

Purple-clay tea holder

Coaster (*Bei Dian*)

The coaster, or cup holder, is used for holding the teacup—aroma cup and appreciation cup—when offering tea. Porcelain or purple-clay coasters are normally used together with the corresponding aroma and appreciation cups, or matching with the bamboo, wood or cloth coaster.

TIPS

● Sometimes coaster are part of the tea ware set, normally six coasters a set.

Carved flower-patterned bamboo slice coaster

Bamboo coaster

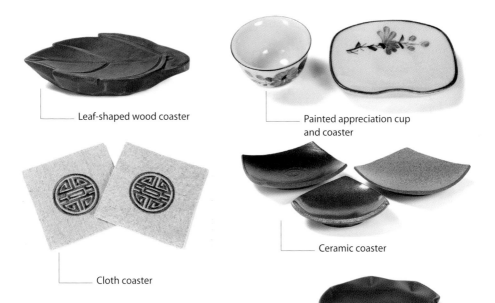

Leaf-shaped wood coaster

Painted appreciation cup and coaster

Cloth coaster

Ceramic coaster

Purple-clay coaster

Tea Serving Tray (*Feng Cha Pan*)

The tea serving tray is normally made of bamboo, wood or porcelain used for placing the teacup when serving tea. Some trays have holders on both sides.

Bamboo tea serving tray

Bamboo tea serving tray

Wooden tea serving tray

Bamboo tea serving tray

Wooden tea serving tray

Porcelain tea serving tray

Bamboo tea serving tray

Porcelain tea serving tray

Tea Props (*Cha Daoju*)

Tea props are the six tools for tea ceremony performance, consisting of the prop holder, tea tong, tea funnel, teaspoon, chaze and tea needle, normally made of bamboo and wood. There are also stainless steel tea tongs.

Wooden tea props

Tea prop holder

The tea prop holder is used for holding the tea tong, tea funnel, teaspoon, chaze and the tea needle.

Tea funnel

The tea funnel is placed on the pot mouth to widen the mouth and prevent the tea leaves from spilling.

Teaspoon

The teaspoon is used for taking out the tea.

Tea needle

The tea needle is used for cleaning the teapot spout.

Chaze

Chaze is used for measuring the quantity of tea.

Tea tong

The tea tong is used for holding the hot cups or picking out the tea dregs.

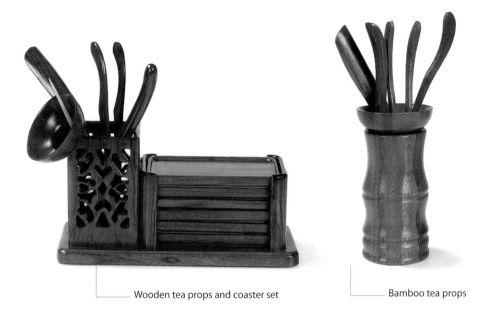

Wooden tea props and coaster set

Bamboo tea props

Pot Brush
(*Yang Hu Bi*)

The pot brush is used to wash the exterior of the purple-clay pot.

Pot brush

Pu-erh Tea Cutter
(*Pu-erh Dao*)

The Pu-erh tea cutter is used to poke and loosen compressed tea. It is a necessary tool for brewing compressed tea.

Pu-erh tea cutter

Tea Canister (*Chaoye Guan*)

It is a container used for storing tea and is made of paper, iron, tin, ceramic and porcelain. The tea canister must be airtight.

TIPS

● Do not store tea in colorless transparent glass canisters.

Tin tea canister

Glass tea canister

Tin tea canister

Green-glazed porcelain tea canister

Stainless steel tea canister

Paper tea canister

Ceramic tea canister

Purple-clay tea canister

Porcelain tea canister

Pot Holder (*Hu Cheng*)

The pot holder is used for holding the pot. It is mostly purple-clay, ceramic and porcelain ware, to match the pot.

Ceramic pot holder

Lid Holder (*Gai Zhi*)

The lid holder is used for holding the pot lid when brewing tea.

Porcelain lid holder

Purple-clay lid holder with separate coaster

Lid holder for the covered bowl lid

Porcelain lid holder

Tea Cloth (*Cha Jin*)

The tea cloth is used to clean water and tea stains from the tea ware. Mostly made of cotton cloth or linen, it should be highly absorbant.

Tea cloth

Tea cloth

Tea cloth

Tea cloth

Water Calyx (*Shui Yu*)

The water calyx is also called the tea calyx, waste water calyx, waste tea calyx. It is used for holding the waste water and tea dregs, and other wastes during the tea appreciation process, normally made of porcelain or pottery.

Ceramic water calyx

Fencai porcelain water calyx

Glass water calyx

Purple-clay calyx

Purple-clay calyx

Doucai porcelain water calyx

Blue-and-white porcelain water calyx

Disinfection Pot (*Xiaodu Guo*)

The disinfection pot is used for sterilizing and cleaning the cups by boiling water and normally sold together with the instant kettle. The disinfection pot is made of stainless steel and often seen in tea shops.

Metal disinfection pot

Pot Cover and Cup Cover (*Hu Tao and Bei Tao*)

The pot and cup covers, made of padded cloth, are used for shielding the pot and cups against damage.

Pot cover

Pot cover

Cup cover

Tea Curios
(*Cha Wan*)

Appreciating tea is not simply a process of brewing to quench thirst, but for the pleasure in the process. Arranging curios on the tea tray, and sharing the tea liquid with them adds to your pleasure, like nourishing the pot. Most curios are made of purple-clay, such as the pig head, foot (symbolizing "always happy" because of the Chinese pronunciation of spider and foot), dogs, golden toads.

Smiling Buddha

Double-fish pendant

Pixiu

Piddling kid

Nine sons of dragon

Happiness

Piglet

Curios representing "always happy"

Tea Sets

Ceramic tea ware

Celadon tea ware

Ceramic tea ware

Purple-clay tea ware

Bone porcelain tea ware

Doucai tea ware

Blue-and-white porcelain tea ware

Portable tea ware with tea tray

Jade color porcelain tea ware

Purple-clay tea ware

PART 3
Tea & Tea Ware

Q&A

Q1. Is black tea made from leaves of the black tea tree?

A: No. Shoots of all kinds of tea trees can be made into black tea, green tea, blue tea, yellow tea, white tea and dark tea. The shoots and leaves of the same tree can be made into green tea with the green tea technique, or black tea with the black tea technique. Only the quality will differ.

Q2. Does the term Long Jing refer only to tea?

A: Long Jing is a name referring to several items. In the southwest mountains in Hangzhou, the origin of West Lake Long Jing, there is the Long Jing Temple, Long Jing Village, Long Jing Spring and Long Jing tea there.

Q3. What does Pu-erh mean?

A: Pu-erh comes from the Hani language, an ethnic group in Yunnan Province. It means a place with water and homes.

Q4. Is black tea called *hei cha* in Chinese?

A: No. the Chinese language calls black tea *hong cha*, which literally means "red tea."

Q5. Which helps to ease the thirst better in summer, iced tea or hot tea?

A: Hot tea.

Q6. Is it Gongfu black tea or Kungfu black tea?

A: As a tea name, it is Gongfu black tea, such as the Qimen Gongfu tea, Dianhong Gongfu tea, etc. Gongfu tea collectively refers to the bar black tea produced in China. The tea-brewing method can be Gongfu tea or Kungfu tea.

Q7. Do all black tea have red leaves as raw material, red liquid and red dregs?

A: No. The tea produced in Darjeeling, India (black tea picked and produced in mid March to mid April), contains only a small quantity of tannin in the leaves and can hardly be fermented with the common black tea fermentation technique. Therefore, the leaves are green.

Q8. What is withering? What is its purpose?

A: Withering is the process of making the brittle fresh tea leaves lose water. The purpose of the process is to partially vaporize the moisture in the leaves, lower the tensibility of the leaf cell, make the peduncle soft and add to the tenacity of the shoot and leaves for twisting and molding. In addition, the leaves experience internal chemical changes laying the foundation for forming different tea types.

Q9. What is twisting? What is its purpose?

A: Twisting is the process of twisting the withered or sun-dried tea leaves under pressure to destroy the tea cells and extract the liquid while rolling the tea leaves into the desired shape. The purpose is to destroy the tea cell to facilitate the necessary oxidation under the function of enzymatic; the tea liquid that comes to the tea-leaf surface increases the flavor and color. Twisting also shapes the shoot and leaves. Twisting can be done by hands or feet, or twisters of different specifications.

Q10. What are the two important sensory indicators of black tea?

A: The golden ring and the turbidity after cooling. There should be a golden ring on the inner wall of the teacup; the thicker the golden ring and stronger the color, the better the tea. The turbidity after cooling refers to the fact that the tea liquid is clear when brewing in the hot water, but becomes turbid after cooling down and the turbidity disappears when the liquid is heated again. The turbidity after cooling is an indicator that the black tea liquid contains rich substances.

Q11. What does fermentation mean? What is its purpose?

A: Fermentation refers to the process of further oxidation of the chemical components of the twisted tea leaves after being piled to a certain thickness in the designated fermentation tray.

Q12. What is Minhong Gongfu Tea?

A: It refers to Gongfu tea produced in Zhenghe, Tanyang and Bailin of Fujian Province.

Q13. What is C.T.C. tea?

A: C.T.C. stands for crushing, tearing and curling. It refers to the tea granule crushed, torn and curled with two rollers of different speed in the tea bar processing. The C.T.C. tea is normally made into tea bags, for instance Lipton black tea. In recent years, Yunnan also produces C.T.C. green tea, in addition to the black tea granule.

Q14. What are the characteristics of the black tea granule?

A: Concentration, intensity and freshness of the taste.

Q15. Where is the extant oldest tea tree? How old is it?

A: The oldest tea tree is found in the wild tea community, Qianjiazhai, Zhenyuan county, Simao, Yunnan Province. It is estimated to be 2,700 years old, by far the oldest one found in the wild.

Q16. What is tribute tea?

A: It is said that the tribute tea started in the tea production area of Sichuan, but became a system in the Tang Dynasty. The tribute tea was the high-quality tea offered to the emperor. In the beginning, the tea was offered by the local officials willingly. But when tea drinking became popular, the demand for the tea tribute increased. The court increased the tea tribute of the states and prefectures on the one hand, and set up the Tea Tribute Institution in Guzhushan (today's Changxing, Huzhou, Zhejiang) in 770 on the other to produce Zisun tribute tea.

Q17. Is Tibet Tea the tea produced in Tibet? Does Tibet produce tea? What tea does it mainly produce?

A: Currently, Tibet Tea distributed in the market is a kind of dark tea, normally compressed. Tibet Tea refers to the tea mainly produced in Ya'an, Sichuan Province and sold to Tibet. Nyingchi, Yiong and Cona of the Tibet Autonomous Region also produce tea, but only a small quantity of green tea, and most of which are consumed locally. The famous tea is Zhufeng Shencha produced in Nyingchi.

Q18. What is Longtuan Fengbing?

A: Longtuan Fengbing is a tea name from the Song Dynasty, also known as the Sliced Tea or Longfeng Tea because the tea cake carried the dragon and phoenix patterns after being compressed in molds.

Q19. What kind of the basic green tea will be fumigated? Why?

A: The baked green tea is the basic green tea to be made into fumigated tea because it is fluffy and easily absorbs the flower fragrance.

Q20. What tea is best in the hot summer?

A: Green tea is recommended in the summer because it is cold in property, can ease one's thirst, relieve the summer heat, detoxify, promote digestion and enhance gastrointestinal functions. In addition, the green tea liquid diminishes inflammation and sterilization. The brewed tea leaves can be used to soak feet to alleviate fatigue and remove odor.

Q21. Is it healthy to drink tea immediately after meals?

A: If you drink tea immediately after meals, the tannic acid in the tea leaves will combine with the protein. It is better to drink one hour after the meal.

Q22: Will the teeth become stained if you drink tea over a long time?

A: Those who are longtime tea drinkers, especially those favoring strong tea, will stain their teeth if they do not pay attention to the dental health. This is because the polyphenol oxides will stick to the tooth surface. Normally brushing teeth twice every day helps. On the contrary, drinking tea will help prevent decayed tooth and strengthen your teeth.

Q23. Is the purple-clay product produced in Yixing only?

A: The purple-clay (also called boccaro pottery) is a kind of clay and only exists in Yixing.

Q24. Can one take medicine with the tea liquid?

A: Normally it is not recommended to take medicine, including traditional Chinese medicine, with the tea liquid, especially medicine containing iron and aluminum because tea affects the absorption of the medicine. However, taking vitamin with the tea liquid will help absorption.

Q25. Can one drink tea during the medication period?

A: Taking medicine does not conflict with drinking tea. But it is recommended not to drink tea two hours before and after medicine. Vitamins are not affected by tea.

Q26. How old does the tea age (*cha shou*) refer to?

A: In China 108 years old is called the tea age because the Chinese character "Cha" (tea) can be interpreted into the numeral 108.

Q27. What do the Two Wonders of the West Lake refer to?

A: Long Jing tea and Hupao Spring Water. Brewing Long Jing tea in the water from the Hupao Spring gives the best flavor.

Q28. Where does the Long Jing tea gets its flat shape from?

A: The friction caused during the process of making Long Jing tea makes the tea flat.

Q29.How many grades does the Long Jing tea have?

A: It is divided into six grades: Special Grade, Grade I, Grade II, Grade III, Grade IV and Grade V.

Q30. How many times can the green tea be re-brewed in a cup?

A: When brewing green tea, the proportion between the tea and water is 1:50. Normally the taste fades after the second and third brewings, especially the top-grade green tea.

Q31. What is the traditional tea-preservation method?

A: Traditionally, lime is used to preserve tea. The newly produced odorless quicklime, packed in clean and odorless paper or cotton cloth, should be placed at the bottom of the container. Place the well-packed tea in the container and seal.

Q32. How many fresh tea leaves will be needed to produce 500g green tea?

A: Normally 2,000g fresh tea leaves can produce 500g dry green tea.

Q33. Some tea, for instance Biluochun and Mengding Ganlu, have too much white fuzz. Do they turn moldy?

A: Some tender tea leaves are often covered with white fuzz. It is an indicator of high quality of the tea, not being moldy.

Q34. Should one drink tea on an empty stomach?

A: It is not good to drink tea, especially the strong one, on an empty stomach. The tea will cause stomach discomfort, sometimes nausea and dizziness or tea drunkenness. Eating candy or drinking hot water can alleviate the condition.

Q35. How much tea is appropriate a day?

A: For a healthy adult, 10g dry tea a day is appropriate. The quantity of tea consumption a day is related to the habit, age, physical condition and living environment. Those who do heavy physical exertion or work on the computer every day and heavy smokers may increase the tea intake appropriately.

Q36. What is fixation? What is its purpose?

A: Fixation refers to the process of destroying enzyme activity of the fresh leaves under the high temperature to stop the enzymatic oxidation of the polyphenol.

Q37. What is Se-enriched tea?

A. The Se-enriched tea refers to the tea with high selenium content. The body requires selenium. In Ziyang of Shaanxi, Fenggang county of Guizhou, Enshi of Hubei, the soil is rich in selenium. Therefore the tea produced there is named Se-enriched tea. Famous Se-enriched tea include Ziyang Maojian and Wuzi Xianhao from Shaanxi.

Q38. Freshly produced green tea is better. Is it better to drink newly made green tea?

A: Before and after the Qingming Festival, famous brands and high-quality green tea are available in the market. In tea-production areas, the green tea is delivered to the consumers on the same day the fresh leaves are picked. However, it is recommended not to drink too much, because of adverse repurcussions from excessive internal heat. Normally the quality of the tea leaves stablizes after a certain period. It is better to store the freshly made green tea for half a month before drinking.

Q39. How to judge whether the water is good for brewing tea?

A: The mineral water that leaves no scales after repeated boiling is appropriate.

Q40. How to prolong the service life of the electric kettle?

A: Do not heat without water, or with the water level too high. Clean the overflowed water and scaling timely.

Q41: Can you brew different kinds of tea in the same pot as long as the pot is appropriate for the tea property?

A: No. The porcelain pot or glass pot can brew different kinds of tea, but each time the teapot should be cleaned. The purple-clay pot is normally used for brewing one kind of tea as it absorbs the flavor of the tea after repeated brewings. Using the purple-clay pot for brewing different kinds of tea will affect the flavor and purity of the taste of the tea. Moreover, the teapot will be more or less spoiled. One purply-clay pot is better for one type of tea only.

Q42. What are the features of the purple-clay pot?

A. The purple-clay pot preserves the natural taste of the tea. A well-nurtured pot can absorb the flavor of tea and give out the tea flavor even without tea. It is highly heat resistant and can withstand slow fire. As it conducts heat slowly, it will not scald the hand while picking it. The different-colored purple-clay pottery has good plasticity. It will not become stale, but exquisite and sleek, and durable. Like antique, pottery made by a famous maker has collection value.

Q43. What is Yanyun of Yancha?

A: Yanyun refers to the unique charm of Wuyi Yancha. Yancha is separated from the others by Yanyun. Whether the tea has Yanyun and whether the Yanyun is excellent are the indicators of the quality of Wuyi Yancha. Yanyun is the flavor of flowers in the rock valley, exclusively owned by the authentic Wuyi Yancha. This essence is the combined effect of the local ecological environment, tea tree variety, planting and management and leaf picking and tea-making process.

Q44. What is "air-conditioned" tea?

A: When producing tea, modern air-conditioning equipment is introduced in the traditional process to control the temperature and humidity of the workshop to increase the quality of the summer tea. The Tieguanyin summer tea in the market is made under air-conditioned environment. The tea is green and has immature taste, inferior to the spring, autumn, and winter teas in terms of the quality.

Q45. What does sun-baked fixation mean?

A: Sun-baked fixation refers to withering of the newly picked fresh tea leaves under the sun. The sun-baking time and thickness of the tea leaf piles vary in different seasons for different kinds of tea leaves and intensity of the sunlight.

Q46. Does Dancong mean a tea tree?

A: Dancong refers to the tea trees with different flavors. The tea leaves are picked up and processed separately according to their flavors. This term does not refer to a unique tea tree.

Q47. How old a tree can be named "ancient tea tree"?

A: Normally, a 100-year or above tree is called an ancient tea tree. According to some, only tea trees older than 360 years can be called ancient.

Q48. What is mellow flavor?

A: The mellow flavor refers to the unique flavor separating Pu-erh tea from the others. The mellow flavor is not the moldy flavor, but the flavor generated in the process of fermentation. There a number of flavors, such as flavor of orchids, Chinese date, camphor tree, lotus and honey and the other flowers and fruits. The Pu-erh tea's orchid flavor is regarded the best.

Q49. Does Qianliangcha weigh 100 jin(50kg)?

A: Qianliangcha, also known as Huajuan tea, was made by businessmen of Shanxi on the lines of Bailiang tea by choosing good raw material, packed and bundled with palm leaves. The column is 166.5cm long with the perimeter 56cm long. It weighs 32.27kg.

Q50. There are codes such as "7572" and "7573" on Pu-erh tea packages. What does it mean?

A: The code is the tea number, or marking. The top right number indicates the code of the tea plant. 1 refers to Kunming Tea Plant, 2 refers to Menghai Tea Plant, 3 Xiaguan Tea Plant, 4 common tea plant. The two numbers on the top left indicate the year of manufacture, the number in the middle refers to the grade of the raw material. 7572 means the Grade 7 Pu-erh tea produced by Menghai Tea Plant and the tea was developed in 1975. The tea code does not indicate the storage time of the tea, but the quality.

Q51. Is it better to store pressed tea or loose leaf tea?

A: Normally, for home storage the compressed Pu-erh tea is chosen because it is smaller in volume and easier to store. And, compared with loose leaf tea, the pressed tea will not deteriorate easily.

Q52. Is Pu-erh tea the older the better?

A: Normally for tea the fresher, the better, especially the green tea. But Pu-erh tea ages better. Each kind of tea has an optimum storage life. When the collected Pu-erh tea reaches its peak, you should enjoy it. If it is stored continuously, the quality will decrease. However, if you collect it as a cultural relic, the longer the better.

Q53. Is artificially fermented Pu-erh tea damp stored tea?

A: The artificially fermented Pu-erh tea is made according to the traditional Pu-erh tea process using a scientific formula of adjusting the water, humidity and air (pile fermentation process). It is different from damp stored tea.

Q54. How to differentiate damp stored tea simply?

A: Damp stored tea looks like the mellow tea, but has an obvious moldy flavor, the liquid in dark red and muddy. It tastes moldy, acidic and bitter. The tea leaves do not unfurl fully. To differentiate it, you can brew the tea for a longer time in boiling water and check the taste.

Q55. Do all Pu-erh tea have collection value?

A: No. Usually, the raw Pu-erh tea has better collection value and potential. With years of storage under the appropriate condition, the raw Pu-erh tea will ferment naturally and the quality will grow better. The ripened tea, or the artificially fermented Pu-erh tea, has fermented in the making process and completed the aging process. There is little value for the long time collection.

Q56. Can the raw tea be drunk directly?

A: Certainly the raw tea can be drunk directly. But the raw tea with a short time of storage is stronger and has an astringent taste. It is recommended to buy the pressed spring tea picked up in the same year. It is soft without bitterness or the astringent taste, and has a lasting aftertaste and strong flavor.

Q57. Is the stronger and darker Pu-erh tea liquid the better?

A: Good-quality Pu-erh tea has clear, red and strong tea liquid. If the tea liquid is too dark and the transparency is bad, then the quality is inferior.

Q58. Why should we use the Pu-erh cutter to loosen the pressed Pu-erh tea?

A: Pu-erh tea is compressed layer by layer. Using the Pu-erh cutter to loosen the tea from one side reduces crumbling.

Q59. Why do some jasmine tea smell of orchid?

A: When the jasmine tea is fumigated, white orchids are used to increase the flavor concentration of the jasmine tea. The quantity of orchid flower should be small. It the quantity is large, the tea will have the flavor of orchid. Sometimes you may find an orchid petal in the dry jasmine tea.

Q60. Is the scented tea better with more dried flower petals?

A: No. High-quality jasmine tea normally has a small amount of flowers. When processing the sweet osmanthus tea, the flowers are not picked out. Some scented tea have a large amount of flowers, known as Banhuacha (tea mixed with flowers). Sometimes dried flower are added to the tea as per the requirements of the consumers. High-quality scented tea has a lasting, fresh and strong flavor of the flower, and tastes excellent.

Reference:

Wang Guangzhi. *Tea of China and Regional Famous Tea*. Beijing: China Agricultural Science and Technology Publishing House, 2003.

Xu Yongcheng. *Famous Mountains Produces Famous Tea*. Beijing: China Agriculture Press, 2003.

Shen Peihe et al. *Tea Assessment Manual*. Beijing: China Agricultural University Press, 1998.

Gong Zhi. *Black Tea of China*. Hangzhou: Zhejiang Photographic Press, 2005.

Hu Xiaojun. *Tea Ware*. Hangzhou: Zhejiang University Press, 2003.

Tea and Tea Set

Acknowledgement

Venue: Beijing Tianyue Tea Company

Ximin Tea

Tea providing: Beijing Gengxiang Tea Co. Ltd.

Puyuan Tea House

Hani Pu-erh (Beijing Office, Yunnan Pu-erh Tea King Co. Ltd.)

Sichuan Yaan Te Plant Co. Ltd. Beijing Office

Zhuoyimu Tea House (Cangshan Tea)

Junshan Yinzhen Tea Co. Ltd.

Xinan Jiufu Tea

Jiaxina Trade Center Black Tea Franchised Shop

Chachan Yipin

Ximin Tea House

Xingtai Tea Shop Yongchun Foshou

Wuyi Mountain Yiren Yancha

Yancha Shop

Anxi Mulin Tieguanyin

Xiaoyang West Lake Longjing

Jiangsu Wuxian County Xishan Biluochun Tea Plant (Fangmeng Tea)

Huangshan Yipinming Tea House

Beijing No.7 Necessity Tea Center

Zhenfeng Tea House

Zhenfengqiao Tea Co. Ltd.

Wang Guangzhi Tea House

Anhui Jinzhai Qifu Organic Tea Plant (Beijing Office)

Contents

FUN DEVOTIONS ABOUT OURSELVES

FUN DEVOTIONS ABOUT OTHERS

Introduction

The enthusiastic response to *Quick Group Devotions for Children's Ministry* highlighted the need for active, quality devotions to help children understand, experience, and apply God's Word.

So here's a new resource filled with 58 devotions to use for children's sermons, Sunday school, junior church, after-school programs, vacation Bible school, day camp—and any other setting where children are gathered.

DEVOTION ELEMENTS

These easy-to-use devotions are based on a variety of scriptures and themes. Each devotion consists of the following elements:

Theme: This is the devotion's topic, the main thought. Themes cover a variety of children's needs and concerns.

Scripture: Each devotion is based on scripture that supports the theme and shows kids that God is concerned about their lives.

Overview: This brief statement describes the devotion and tells what the children will learn.

Preparation: This part describes exactly what materials you'll need for the devotion and what you'll need to do to prepare.

Experience: Each devotion contains a unique element that lets children actually experience the theme. Kids use their senses of sight, hearing, smell, touch, and taste to understand the topic.

All activities can be adapted to fit your group's size. If you have a small group, do the devotional activities together. If your group is larger, divide into small groups. For example, you can divide into small groups by height or birthdays.

Response: Children think about what they've experienced and how it applies to their lives.

Closing: Each devotion concludes with a prayer or activity that summarizes the devotional thought and helps children apply it to their lives.

Be creative and have a good time with *Fun Group Devotions for Children's Ministry*. Adapt and use these ready-to-go devotions any time and anywhere—to share fun, meaningful times that lead your children into deeper walks with God.

Section 1:
FUN DEVOTIONS ABOUT FAITH

WISHING WELL PRAYERS

● **THEME:** Prayer

● **SCRIPTURE:** Psalm 91:15-16

● **OVERVIEW:** Children toss pennies into a large container and learn the difference between wishes and prayer.

● **PREPARATION:** For each person you'll need 10 pennies. You'll also need a Bible and a large bowl or basket.

EXPERIENCE

Place the large bowl in the center of the room. Have children sit in a circle around the bowl, about 4 feet away. Give each person 10 pennies.

Say: **This bowl is a wishing well. For each of your pennies, make a wish, then toss the penny in the well. Your wish is supposed to come true if your penny lands in the well. If the penny lands outside the well, don't pick it up—just leave it.**

RESPONSE

After kids have tossed their 10 pennies, ask: **How did you feel making wishes with this wishing well? What's the difference between a wishing well and a prayer? Can the wishing well really hear and answer your wishes? Why or why not?**

Read aloud Psalm 91:15-16.

Ask: **Does God hear us when we call upon him? Will he answer us? Why or why not?**

Say: **God wants a relationship with us. He wants to know all about us—our problems, what we wish for, and what we think and feel. God wants us to follow him.**

CLOSING

Ask kids to each retrieve 10 pennies from the bowl or the floor. Say: **Now let's offer God a "penny prayer." For each penny, say one thing you're thankful for, such as family or friends. Toss the penny in the bowl after you give thanks.**

Close by praying: **Lord, thanks for hearing our prayers and for being better than any wishing well. Please teach us to hear your voice and follow you. Amen.**

Collect the pennies and place them in the Sunday school offering.

"I TOLD YOU NOT TO TOUCH THAT!"

- ● **THEME:** Temptation
- ● **SCRIPTURE:** Matthew 4:1-11
- ● **OVERVIEW:** Children go on a "temptation scavenger hunt" to learn about temptation. (Best for upper-elementary kids.)
- ● **PREPARATION:** You'll need a Bible, paper, and pencils.

EXPERIENCE

Read aloud Matthew 4:1-11. Ask: **What does it mean to be tempted by something? Do you sometimes feel like someone is trying to get you to do something wrong, like Satan tried to get Jesus to do? Why or why not?**

Give each person a sheet of paper and a pencil. Say: **We're going on a temptation scavenger hunt. We'll walk around the church and look for things that could be tempting to us. Each time you see something tempting, such as a bowl of candy or art supplies in a classroom, write down or draw a picture of the temptation, but don't take the item. Come back to our room in five minutes.**

After five minutes, gather everyone back together.

RESPONSE

Ask kids to tell what they wrote or drew on their papers. Ask: **What surprises you about these lists? Were you tempted to touch the items you found? Why or why not? Do you think most people are tempted by the things on our papers? Why or why not? Why didn't you give in to temptation when you felt it? Why do you think Jesus resisted Satan's temptations? What's the best way to resist temptations?**

CLOSING

Have kids pick the strongest temptation on their papers. Then ask them to each write under that temptation one way they can resist it in the future. For example, if the temptation is to cheat at school, someone might write, "I'll work harder in school, so I won't be tempted to cheat." Form pairs and have partners tell each other how they plan to resist temptation.

Ask partners to join hands. Pray: **God, give us strength to resist temptations. Help us follow Jesus' example. Amen.**

POWER SOURCE

● **THEME:** God's power
● **SCRIPTURE:** Acts 1:8
● **OVERVIEW:** Children inflate balloons and compare that to God's power through the Holy Spirit.
● **PREPARATION:** For each person you'll need a balloon. You'll also need a Bible, tape, and ribbon.

EXPERIENCE

Hand each person a deflated balloon. Give kids one minute to toss their deflated balloons as far as they can. Allow them to toss the deflated balloons as many times as they can during the minute.

Next, give kids two minutes to inflate their balloons (without tying them off) and release them to sail around the room. Help those who can't inflate their balloons. Encourage kids to inflate and release their balloons several times.

RESPONSE

After two minutes, have kids pick up their balloons and sit down in a circle. Ask: **When did your balloons sail the farthest—when they were deflated or when they were filled with air? What gave the balloons power?**

Read aloud Acts 1:8. Ask: **What fills Christians with power? What is every Christian's job? How do you think God feels when Christians won't let the Holy Spirit fill their lives with power?**

Say: **God promises to fill Christians with the Holy Spirit so they can have power to tell others about Jesus. Sometimes people are like our deflated balloons. They are powerless because they don't allow the Holy Spirit to enter them. God is happy when he can fill us with the Holy Spirit and give us power to tell others about Jesus.**

CLOSING

Have kids inflate and tie their balloons. Use ribbon to tie the balloons together in a balloon bouquet. Have kids take turns batting the balloon bouquet in the air. With each "bat," have kids say one word in the following sentence: "Holy Spirit, thanks for your power."

For two or three minutes, continue batting the bouquet and saying words to the sentence over and over. Then tape the bouquet near the meeting room door. Each time kids enter or leave the room, they'll remember God sent the Holy Spirit to fill them with power.

4 AWESOME GOD

● **THEME:** Faith
● **SCRIPTURE:** Ephesians 3:20-21
● **OVERVIEW:** Children make a choice and learn about God's awesome power.
● **PREPARATION:** You'll need 20 inches of heavy string, a wastebasket, two tennis balls, and a Bible.

EXPERIENCE

Choose two children. Tie one person's hands behind his or her back. Give each of these two children a tennis ball. Tell them to stand 10 feet away from the wastebasket and toss their balls into the basket. They can have as many tries as they need.

Then stop the kids before they start throwing. Ask the observers to stand behind the person they think can actually get the ball in the wastebasket.

Ask: **Why did you choose the person you did? Which person do you have faith in? Explain. What is faith?**

RESPONSE

Untie the one child's hands. Have all kids sit down in a circle. Then read aloud Ephesians 3:20-21. Ask: **What does it mean that God is "able to do much, much more than anything we can ask or imagine"? Is God more like the person with tied-up hands or the person with free hands? Explain. According to these verses, what are good reasons to have faith in God?**

CLOSING

Go around the circle and have kids thank God for one thing he can do that seems impossible, such as making an earthquake stop. Celebrate the faith your kids express by having them say, "Yea, God" after each item.

UNWORLDLY WORSHIP

● **THEME:** Worship

● **SCRIPTURE:** Matthew 4:10; John 9:31

● **OVERVIEW:** Children act out what people worship in everyday life, then brainstorm ways they can worship God. (Best for upper-elementary kids.)

● **PREPARATION:** You'll need a Bible, paper, pencils, slips of paper, magazines, and a hat or bowl.

EXPERIENCE

Form groups of no more than three. Give each group paper, a pencil, and a magazine. Ask: **What does it mean to worship someone or something? If you wanted to worship someone or something, how would you do it? Besides God, what are things people worship in their lives?**

Say: **As a group, look through your magazine and find someone or something that people worship. Then decide how your group can pantomime—act without speaking—how people worship that person or thing. For example, you might find a picture of expensive jewelry. Each person in your group could pantomime showing off flashy rings, bracelets, and necklaces. You have five minutes to think of an idea and be ready to present it.**

After five minutes, have the groups each present their pantomime. Ask the rest of the kids to guess what each group is portraying.

RESPONSE

Ask: **How did you feel pantomiming what people worship in everyday life? Why do people worship the things they do? What do you worship in your life?**

Read aloud Matthew 4:10. Ask: **According to this verse, who should you worship?**

CLOSING

Give each group a slip of paper and a pencil.

Read aloud John 9:31. Ask: **What does this verse promise God will do when we worship him?**

Say: **God listens to us when we worship and obey him. In your group, think of one way you can worship God during the next week, such as go to church, pray daily, or sing songs. Write your idea on your slip of paper.**

Collect the slips of paper in a hat. Mix the slips and redistribute them so groups don't receive the ones they wrote.

Ask each group to read the worship idea, then have group members sign their names to the slip of paper as a promise to do what their slip says during the next week.

ZIGZAGGING THROUGH LIFE

● **THEME:** God's guidance

● **SCRIPTURE:** Proverbs 4:25–5:1

● **OVERVIEW:** Children run a zigzag race and learn about following a straight path to God.

● **PREPARATION:** You'll need a Bible and six boxes.

EXPERIENCE

Ask kids to help you position six boxes for a relay (see example on page 17). Form two teams. Have them line up on one side of the boxes. Say: **On "go," the first person in each team zigzags around the boxes and back, then tags the next person who zigzags, and so on. The first team to finish wins.**

Demonstrate the zigzag, then say: **Ready? Go!**

Clap for the winning team, then say: **Now, repeat the race, but**

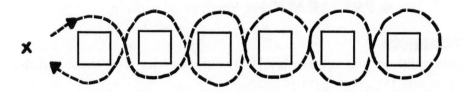

this time, don't zigzag. **Run straight to the opposite side of the room, touch your last box, and then run back and tag the next person in line. The first team to finish wins. Ready? Go!**

Clap for the winning team.

RESPONSE

Have children sit in a circle. **Ask: Which race went the fastest— the zigzag or running straight to the last box and back? Explain.**

Say: **Listen to what the Bible says about straight paths.**

Read aloud Proverbs 4:25–5:1. Ask: **What advice does this passage give us? How can we stay on the "road of goodness"?**

CLOSING

Ask kids to line up behind you. Lead them in "looking straight ahead" and walking a straight path across the room and back. As you walk, ask kids to call out ways to seek God's guidance, such as praying and listening to teachers and pastors.

Have kids sit on the boxes, close their eyes, and listen as you pray: **Lord, guide us each day on the straight, good path that leads right to you. Amen.**

OKAY, I'LL OBEY

- ● **THEME:** Obedience
- ● **SCRIPTURE:** 1 John 5:3-5
- ● **OVERVIEW:** Children follow a leader and learn about obedience.

● **PREPARATION:** You'll need a Bible.

EXPERIENCE

Have children line up to play Follow the Leader. Tell them to follow you and do everything you do.

Lead kids around the room hopping on one foot, turning circles, waving, or clapping. After a minute, ask a volunteer to be the next leader. Give several children the chance to lead.

RESPONSE

Have kids sit in a circle. Ask: **How did you feel as you followed the leader? How is this like the way you feel when you try to obey God?**

Read aloud 1 John 5:3-5. Ask: **What does this passage tell us about obeying God?**

Say: **If we love God, we'll obey his commands. God gives us the Holy Spirit to help us follow his commands.**

CLOSING

Have kids stand in a circle. Say: **I command you to put your arms around each other's shoulders. Now, lift one foot in the air and balance on the other foot. Hold this position while I'll pray.**

Pray: **Dear God, just like we obeyed and are standing like this for this prayer, help us obey your commands in our lives. Thank you for Jesus. Amen.**

Have kids resume normal positions as they continue to obey God this next week!

LOVE UNLIMITED

● **THEME:** Valentine's Day
● **SCRIPTURE:** John 13:34
● **OVERVIEW:** Children observe lighted candles

and learn that God's love is limitless.

● **PREPARATION:** For each person you'll need a birthday candle and a handful of clay. You'll also need a Bible, a large candle, and matches.

EXPERIENCE

Use this devotion on Valentine's Day or any day you want to talk about God's love.

Give each child a handful of clay and a birthday candle. Ask kids to each form their clay into a heart shape, then poke their candle into the clay. Each person now has a candle stand.

Rather than sitting in a circle, have children sit in a heart shape with their candles in front of them. As the children watch you, use the large candle to light each child's candle, one at a time.

RESPONSE

Read aloud John 13:34. Ask: **How did the fire spread from the light of one candle? How is God's love like the flame in the large candle?**

Say: **God asks us to love one another as he loves us. God wants us to spread his never-ending love to others.**

CLOSING

Have kids each tell one way they'll spread God's love to others this week; for example, "hug them" or "be nice to new people in school."

Have kids blow out their candles. Encourage them to place their heart-shaped candle on the kitchen table to remind them to share God's love with everyone—not just on Valentine's Day, but every day.

TRUST-MATES

● **THEME:** Trust
● **SCRIPTURE:** Proverbs 3:5-6

● **OVERVIEW:** Children must choose who to trust while following directions to a pirate's treasure.

● **PREPARATION:** You'll need a Bible, wrapped candy, and markers. Hide a collection of wrapped candy (the treasure) somewhere in your room. Have enough extra candy so everyone can have a piece during the closing.

EXPERIENCE

Form three groups—the "pirates," the "first mates," and the "second mates." Ask all pirates to wait outside the room and cover their ears while you give directions to the first and second mates.

Show all first and second mates where the treasure is hidden. Quietly tell the first mates: **Your job is to truthfully tell the pirates where the treasure is. If the pirates listen to you and find the treasure, they'll share the goodies with you.** Ask all first mates to stand in one corner of the room.

Then, quietly tell the second mates: **Your job is to confuse the pirates by telling them that the treasure is someplace else. If you can confuse the pirates long enough, you'll win the treasure all by yourselves.** Ask all second mates to stand in another corner of the room.

Tell all first and second mates not to shout out their directions until you say, "Shiver me timbers!"

Bring in the pirates, then say: **Pirates, when I call out "Shiver me timbers!" the first and second mates will tell you where to find an incredible treasure. You must find the treasure in 30 seconds, or it'll be lost forever. The first and second mates can't go to the treasure themselves; they can only shout out directions. Ready? Shiver me timbers!**

RESPONSE

If the first mates succeed in guiding the pirates to the treasure, let them share the candy. If the second mates succeed in confusing the pirates, let the second mates eat the treasure themselves.

Ask: **Pirates, was it hard to know who to trust? Why or why not? How did you decide who to trust? Everyone, how is this game like trusting people in real life?**

Read aloud Proverbs 3:5-6. Ask: **Is it easier to trust people or to trust God? Explain. What's one way you can trust God for something? What does it mean when the Bible says God will "give you success" if you trust him?**

CLOSING

Give kids each a marker and a piece of wrapped candy. Ask kids to each think of something they have a hard time trusting God for, such as safety of family members. Have them each unwrap their candy and write on the wrapper the reference "Proverbs 3:5-6." Then have them eat their candy, keeping the wrapper to take home.

Reread Proverbs 3:5-6, then say: **When you're struggling to trust God, look up the Bible reference written on your candy wrapper. Remember God's wise advice to trust him with all your heart.**

GIVE IT UP

- ● **THEME:** Giving
- ● **SCRIPTURE:** Luke 21:1-4
- ● **OVERVIEW:** Children play a game and learn what it really means to give.
- ● **PREPARATION:** You'll need a Bible.

EXPERIENCE

Have children sit in a circle. Ask them to each give something to the person on their right. The object they give must be something they have with them or on them. Children may choose things such as a piece of lint, a penny, a pen, or a strand of hair.

Ask: **How did you decide what to give? Why do we sometimes give something because we don't need it or care about it anymore?**

Say: **Let's listen to a story about a woman who gave away her last two coins.**

RESPONSE

Read aloud Luke 21:1-4. Ask: **How did our giving compare to how the widow gave?**

Say: **Even though the widow's gift was small, Jesus said it was worth more than any other because she gave up something she really needed.**

Ask: **How we can give to others like the widow gave to God?**

Go around the circle. One at a time, have kids tell one way they'll give to others this next week, such as "I'll give some time to my little brother and help him with his schoolwork."

CLOSING

Close by having each person "give" a compliment to the person on his or her right, such as "You're a good friend."

Then pray and give Jesus thanks for all he's given us.

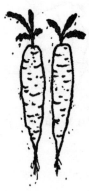

HE IS RISEN

● **THEME:** Easter

● **SCRIPTURE:** John 20:1-18

● **OVERVIEW:** Children watch an inanimate object "come to life" and learn how the disciples might have felt when Jesus rose from the dead.

● **PREPARATION:** For each person, you'll need a straw in a wrapper (available at fast-food restaurants) and a pin. You'll also need a Bible, tape, scissors, and a glass of water.

EXPERIENCE

Say: **Today you're going to see something that's "dead" come to life again.**

Gather kids around a glass of water and give each one a straw in a wrapper. Have kids each tear off the very top of the wrapper, then carefully scrunch down the wrapper to the bottom (it should look like an accordion or a crumpled worm). Then have them slide their "crumpled worm" off the straw and put it on the floor in front of them. Have each person dip a finger in the glass, then sprinkle a few drops of water on his or her wrapper. The wrapper will "grow" when water hits it.

RESPONSE

Read aloud John 20:1-18. Ask: **How did you feel when I promised you'd get to see something dead come to life again? Were you surprised when your wrapper moved? Why or why not? How do you think Jesus' followers felt when they saw him alive again? If you had been there, how would you have reacted?**

Say: **Jesus warned those close to him that he would have to die to save them from their sins. But he also promised them he would live again. It must have been hard to trust what Jesus said. But he came through on his promise!**

CLOSING

Supply scissors and tape. Give each person a pin. Have kids cut their straws about one-third down from the top. Then have them tape the two pieces into a cross. Help kids each pin their cross onto their shirt.

Together, shout, "Jesus is alive!"

FRESH STARTS

● **THEME:** Starting over

● **SCRIPTURE:** 2 Timothy 4:7-8a

● **OVERVIEW:** Children run a race and experience fresh starts.

● **PREPARATION:** For each person, you'll need a sheet of paper and a piece of candy. You'll also need a Bible.

EXPERIENCE

Give each person a sheet of paper. Have kids line up on one side of the room. Tell them to each hold out their right hand, palm up, fingers spread apart. Have them each balance their paper on their fingertips. Say: **On "go," balance your paper while walking to the opposite side of the room and back. If the paper falls off, just stop, put the paper back on your fingertips, and keep going until you finish the race. Ready? Go!**

RESPONSE

After kids finish, have them sit down in a circle. Say: **Congratulations! No matter how many times you dropped your paper, you picked it up and kept going. Good job. You all get a reward.**

Give each person a piece of candy. Ask: **How did you feel during the race? How would you have felt if you had to go all the way back to the beginning each time you dropped the paper?**

Read aloud 2 Timothy 4:7-8a. Ask: **How are our feelings after our race like Timothy's feelings in this passage? What was Timothy's reward for finishing his race?**

Say: **Timothy said he fought a good fight and kept the faith. Just like we picked up our papers and kept going in our race, God helps us pick up the pieces after difficult times and keep going in life. God helps us start over.**

CLOSING

Have kids hold hands in the circle. Pray: **God, thanks for always loving us, forgiving us, and giving us fresh starts in life. Help us "fight a good fight" during life and keep the faith. Amen.**

 # REACHING FOR GOD

● **THEME:** Knowing God
● **SCRIPTURE:** Romans 3:23-24

● **OVERVIEW:** Children throw drinking straws and learn we can never reach God through our own efforts.

● **PREPARATION:** For each person you'll need a drinking straw. You'll also need a Bible.

EXPERIENCE

Give each person a straw. Have kids line up against one wall. Say: **We're going to practice throwing our straws. I'll tell you how far to try. First, throw your straw as far as you can.** (Pause) **Go get your straw and try it again.** (Pause) **Now, throw your straw as high as you can.** (Pause) **Get your straw. One more time, throw it as high as you can.**

RESPONSE

Have kids get their straws and sit in a circle. Ask: **How did you feel about your efforts to throw your straws? Which straw was thrown the farthest? highest? Who could throw their straw far enough to hit a cloud? a passing airplane? heaven? How is trying to throw our straws like trying to reach God on our own? Can people be good enough to reach God on their own? Why or why not?**

Read aloud Romans 3:23-24. Ask: **Why aren't we "good enough for God's glory"? How can we reach God? What did Jesus do for us?**

CLOSING

Ask children to keep their drinking straws to remind them that Jesus is the way to heaven.

Have kids join hands and bow their heads. Pray: **Lord, thanks for reaching down to us when we could not reach high enough to reach you. Thanks for your forgiveness and love. Amen.**

14 THE SWEET TASTE OF THANKS

● **THEME:** Thanksgiving
● **SCRIPTURE:** 1 Chronicles 16:8-10
● **OVERVIEW:** Children taste unsweetened Kool-Aid and learn what life without giving thanks is like.
● **PREPARATION:** For each person, you'll need two cups. You'll also need a Bible, a pitcher filled with unsweetened Kool-Aid, a pitcher filled with water, a packet of unsweetened Kool-Aid, a measuring cup, a teaspoon, a long-handled spoon, and a canister of sugar.

EXPERIENCE

Use this devotion near Thanksgiving or any time you want to talk about giving God thanks.

Give kids each a cup of unsweetened Kool-Aid. (Don't tell them what it is.) Have them wait to drink until everyone is served. Say: **Since our snack is just something to drink, not anything too important, I don't think it's necessary to give thanks for it. Go ahead and drink it.**

Ask: **What's wrong with the drink? What was wrong about not giving thanks?**

Say: **Life without thanks is like a sip of unsweetened Kool-Aid. It has a flavor, but it's sure not sweet. Allow kids to pour their drink back into the pitcher.**

Say: **Let's start from the beginning.**

RESPONSE

Bring out a pitcher filled with water, a packet of unsweetened Kool-Aid, a measuring cup, a teaspoon, a long-handled spoon, and a canister of sugar.

Read aloud 1 Chronicles 16:8-10. Say: **Let's practice giving thanks to God. For each thanks you express, you can put one** teaspoon of sugar into the measuring cup. When the cup is full, we'll stir it with the unsweetened Kool-Aid into the pitcher of water.

Let kids take turns giving thanks. Once the cup is full of sugar, add it and the Kool-Aid mix to the pitcher of water. Have kids take turns stirring the new mixture. Pour each person a cup and let kids each take one sip.

Ask: **What's different about this sip of Kool-Aid? How can giving thanks add sweetness to our lives?**

CLOSING

Have kids each say a sentence prayer of thanks, then drink the rest of his or her sweetened Kool-Aid.

GOD'S LOVE IN OUR HEART

● **THEME:** God's love

● **SCRIPTURE:** John 15:13-17

● **OVERVIEW:** Children decorate posters and learn about God's love.

● **PREPARATION:** For each person, you'll need a red construction paper heart. You'll also need tape, butcher paper, crayons, and a Bible.

EXPERIENCE

Measure one sheet of butcher paper for the length of each child from the waist up. Use a crayon and trace each child's torso on the butcher paper. For older children, have them pair up and trace each other's outlines on butcher paper.

Supply crayons. Have kids each decorate their outline to resemble themselves right now—same color hair, eyes, and clothes. As kids are drawing, go around and tape a red construction paper heart to each child's drawing. Write on the heart "God's love fills (*name*)'s heart."

RESPONSE

When kids finish, have them tape their posters to the meeting room wall. Ask: **What is different about our posters? What is the same?**

Say: **Each one of our posters is different, just like each one of us is different. The thing that is the same is that our hearts are filled with God's love. Let's hear a Bible passage that says more about God's love.**

Read aloud John 15:13-17. Ask: **What does Jesus command us to do?**

Say: **Even though God has given us many different talents, abilities, and appearances, the most important thing about us is the same—God's love in our hearts. Because God loves us, we love each other.**

CLOSING

Have kids stand in front of their posters, place their hand over their hearts, and repeat each line of this prayer after you:
Dear God,
Thanks for making me special.
Thanks for your love in my heart.
Help me love others.
Like you love me.
Amen.

PRAISE PAIRS

● **THEME:** Praise
● **SCRIPTURE:** Philippians 4:8
● **OVERVIEW:** Children race to list things about each other that are good and "praiseworthy."

● **PREPARATION:** You'll need a Bible, newsprint, paper, pencils, markers, tape, and a table.

EXPERIENCE

Tape newsprint to a wall in a central place. Write the following words on the newsprint: true, honorable, right, pure, beautiful, respected.

Read aloud Philippians 4:8. Then say: **This scripture tells us to think of things that are good and "worthy of praise." What are some foods that are good and worthy of praise?**

Have kids call out good foods, then say: **When I say "go," walk around the room telling others your favorite food. Find someone else who likes the same food as you, then sit down together. Ready? Go!**

After a minute or two, have kids stop. Make sure everyone has a partner. Have partners tell each other why their favorite food is good and worthy of praise.

Give each pair a sheet of paper and a pencil. Say: **With your partner, you have two minutes to think of as many things about each other that are good and worthy of praise. You can use this list of words from Philippians 4:8** (point to the newsprint list) **to help you think. Write each praiseworthy thing about each other on your paper. The pair that comes up with the most praiseworthy things about each other wins!**

After two minutes, call time and ask pairs, one by one, to stand together and read aloud their praiseworthy list. Count the number for each pair, then declare a winning pair. Have the group surround the pair and give them a standing ovation.

RESPONSE

Ask: **Was it easy or hard to think of things to praise about your partner? about yourself? Explain. How did it feel to praise someone? to be praised? Why do you think God asks us to think about things that are good and worthy of praise?**

CLOSING

Say: **We found plenty of reasons to praise one another. Now let's find reasons to praise God.**

Have kids find something inside or outside your meeting room that was created by God and is worthy of praise, such as a plant or a picture of a friend or parent.

Have kids bring their praiseworthy things and sit in a circle. One at a time, have kids thank God for their item. Place all praiseworthy items on a table. On a sheet of paper write "Thanks, God, for these good and praiseworthy gifts." Tape the sign above the table. Leave the display in your room as a reminder of the lesson.

EXPECTING GREAT THINGS

- **THEME:** Anticipation
- **SCRIPTURE:** Mark 10:46-52
- **OVERVIEW:** Children watch a jack-in-the-box toy and learn good things are going to happen.
- **PREPARATION:** You'll need a Bible and a jack-in-the-box pop-up toy (look for this toy in your church nursery or purchase an inexpensive one at a toy store).

EXPERIENCE

Have kids sit down in a circle. Show the jack-in-the-box toy. Ask: **If I wind this toy, what do you expect will happen? Why do you think a toy will pop out?**

Most kids will expect the toy to pop out because of their past experiences with similar toys.

Wind the toy and watch what happens. Try it several times, letting other kids wind the toy.

RESPONSE

Ask: **How is the way we knew the jack-in-the-box would pop out like the way we know Jesus will keep his promises to us?**

Say: **Let's read about a man who knew Jesus would heal him.**

He knew about Jesus' healing people before him, and he knew Jesus could heal him, too. The man believed in Jesus. He expected great things to happen.

Read aloud Mark 10:46-52.

CLOSING

Go around the circle. Ask kids to each say one good thing God has done for them in the past, such as "God healed me when I was very sick." Next, ask kids to each say one good thing they expect God will do for them in the future, such as "God will help me face my problems."

Tell kids they're going to say a pop-up prayer. Wind the pop-up toy. When the toy pops up, "pop up" and thank God for one blessing or gift you've been given, such as "Thanks God for the gift of a good family." Pass the toy to the person on your right and have him or her repeat the process. Continue until everyone has given a pop-up prayer.

AN "ORDINARY" CHRISTMAS?

- ● **THEME:** Christmas
- ● **SCRIPTURE:** Luke 2:1-20
- ● **OVERVIEW:** Children create a manger scene from ordinary things in the room.
- ● **PREPARATION:** You'll need a Bible, tape, paper, pipe cleaners, a candle, and matches.

EXPERIENCE

Say: **Something big is about to happen. All the stores are decorated, there's excitement in the air, and people are looking forward to celebrating with their families.**

Ask: **Who knows what this big thing is? Why do you think**

we make such a big deal about Christmas? What's Christmas really all about, anyway?

Read aloud Luke 2:1-20. Then say: **Christmas is about the birth of Jesus. Maybe you have a manger scene in your home.**

Ask: **What do most manger scenes show?**

Say: **Now that we have some ideas, let's make our own manger scene out of "ordinary" objects in our meeting room. You also can use the paper, tape, and pipe cleaners if you need them.** Kids could use a large cardboard box for the stable and a Kleenex tissues box for a manger. They could use pencils and chalkboard erasers for the manger scene figures and decorate them with paper, tape, and pipe cleaners.

When kids find ordinary objects to use in their creation, have them bring the objects to the center of the room. Then have kids work together to make a manger scene using all of the objects.

RESPONSE

After kids complete the manger scene, ask: **How does our manger scene compare to ones you've seen at home or in the store? How does Jesus' birth compare to the way other kings are born? Why did God choose to have Jesus' birth take place in such an ordinary place, surrounded by such ordinary people? How did this activity make you feel about Christmas?**

Say: **Christmas is really a celebration of Jesus' birthday. But sometimes it's easy to forget "the reason for the season."**

Ask: **How would you feel if all your friends came to your birthday party but forgot why they came? How do you think God feels when we forget what happened in that ordinary manger? How can we show God we haven't forgotten the reason for the season?**

CLOSING

Have kids gather around the homemade manger scene. Light one candle, then turn off all the lights. Together, sing "Away in the Manger." Then ask kids to silently pray for Jesus to show them one way they can celebrate the real meaning of Christmas.

ALKA-SELTZERED BALLOONS

- **THEME:** The Holy Spirit
- **SCRIPTURE:** 1 Corinthians 6:19-20; Ephesians 5:18-20
- **OVERVIEW:** Children combine water and an Alka-Seltzer tablet in a balloon, creating a visual image of how God lives in us.
- **PREPARATION:** You'll need a Bible, several paper cups filled with water, Alka-Seltzer tablets, small 5-inch balloons, and kitchen funnels.

EXPERIENCE

Form groups of no more than three. Give each group a cup of water, an Alka-Seltzer tablet, a balloon, and a kitchen funnel. Have one person from each group insert the Alka-Seltzer tablet into the balloon. Have another person insert the funnel into the balloon's mouth. Have the third person pour water through the funnel and into the balloon, then tie the balloon closed.

Watch what happens to the balloons!

RESPONSE

Have kids sit down in a circle. Ask: **What happened when you combined Alka-Seltzer and water in your balloon? How did you feel when you watched it happen? How are the expanding balloons like us when we're filled with God's love?**

Read aloud 1 Corinthians 6:19-20 and Ephesians 5:18-20. Ask: **How can we be filled with the Holy Spirit?**

Say: **This passage says we receive the Holy Spirit from God. We should sing, make music in our hearts to God, and always give thanks for everything. The Holy Spirit may be invisible, but like the fizz in the Alka-Seltzer, we know the Holy Spirit lives in us.**

CLOSING

Give each child an empty balloon. Say: **We are like empty balloons unless we receive the Holy Spirit from God.** Help kids
inflate and tie their balloons. Then say: **When the Holy Spirit lives
in us, we are filled with thankfulness and joy. Let's pray now.
Each one of you say anything you're thankful for. At the end of
the prayer, we'll walk to the middle of the circle, bop balloons
together, and shout "Amen!"**

Section 2:
FUN DEVOTIONS ABOUT OURSELVES

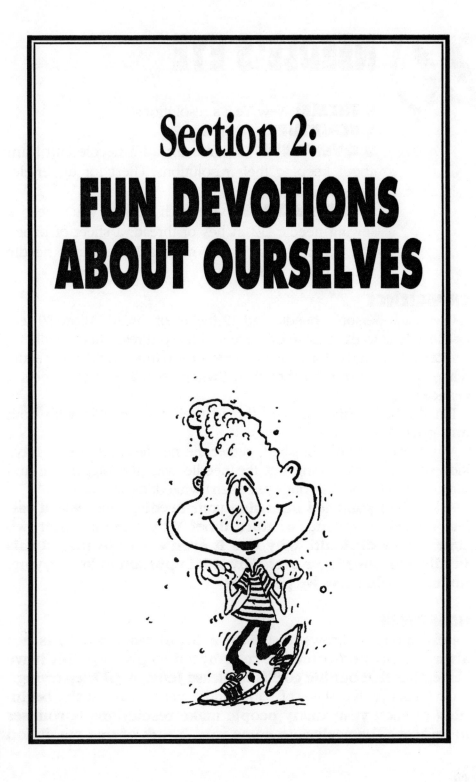

20 NEEDLE'S EYE

● **THEME:** New Year's resolutions

● **SCRIPTURE:** Hebrews 12:1

● **OVERVIEW:** Children thread a needle and learn about keeping their resolutions. (Best for upper-elementary kids.)

● **PREPARATION:** For each person, you'll need a sewing needle, 12 inches of thread, a sheet of paper, and a pencil. You'll also need a Bible and a needle with a bigger eye.

EXPERIENCE

Give each person a needle and 12 inches of thread. Allow 30 seconds for kids to each close one eye and try to thread their needle.

After 30 seconds, form pairs. Have one partner hold the needle while the other tries to thread it. Switch so that everyone gets a chance to try.

Finally, have children each thread their own needle with both eyes open.

When everyone has finished, gather the needles and thread. Have kids sit in a circle. Bring out the needle with the bigger eye and thread it (with both of your eyes open) while kids watch.

Ask: **When you tried threading your needle, when was it easiest—the first, second, or third time? Why were the first two times more difficult? Why was it even easier to thread this needle with the bigger eye? Why is it important to keep trying, no matter what task we perform?**

RESPONSE

Read aloud Hebrews 12:1. Say: **A lot of work we do is not always easy, and often we're tempted to give up. But if we remember that our big goal is to please Jesus, we'll keep trying.**

Give kids each a sheet of paper and a pencil. Say: **At the beginning of each year, many people make resolutions—promises to improve themselves in some way. Think of one resolution** you want to make. It could be "I will read my Bible every day" or "I will willingly help with chores." Write your resolution on your paper.

CLOSING

Have kids get with their partners again. Have partners read their resolutions to each other.

Reread Hebrews 12:1. Pray: **Lord, help us work the best we can. Help us keep our resolutions and never give up. We are serving you. Amen.**

ANGER EXERCISES

● **THEME:** Anger
● **SCRIPTURE:** Ephesians 4:26-27
● **OVERVIEW:** Children practice constructive ways to deal with anger.
● **PREPARATION:** You'll need a Bible.

EXPERIENCE

Form pairs. Say: **Think of things that make you really, really mad, such as people making fun of you. Take two minutes and talk about those things with your partner.**

After two minutes, have partners take turns yelling the things they talked about in an angry tone.

Say: **Those situations really do make us mad. Sometimes we deal with our anger by hitting, yelling, or calling people names. What other ways do we hurt others, ourselves, or things around us when we're angry?**

Read aloud Ephesians 4:26-27. Say: **God doesn't say it's wrong to be angry. But he _is_ concerned with how we handle our anger. Let's practice a few ideas to help us handle our anger without hurting anyone or anything.**

RESPONSE

Have kids imagine one thing that makes them really, really angry. Then lead them in practicing these positive ways to deal with anger:

● **The one-minute growl**—Say: **Start growling, quietly at first, then get louder and stronger. Finally, break into howling or barking.**

After one minute, ask: **Does anyone still feel as angry as when you started? Why or why not?**

● **The bug stomp**—Say: **Imagine whatever is making you angry is a bug running across the floor. Stomp on it, stomp on it, stomp on it! Grind it, mash it, and jump on it till it's gone.**

After one minute, ask: **Does anyone still feel as angry as when you started? Why or why not?**

● **Mean faces**—Say: **Make the meanest, most angry face you can. Snarl, growl, and show your teeth. Try to keep from laughing— remember you're angry!**

After one minute, ask: **Does anyone still feel as angry as when you started? Why or why not?**

● **Move the wall**—Say: **Stand against the wall and push. Push as hard as you can with your hands, your back, and your head. Growl at the same time if you're angry enough.**

After one minute, ask: **Does anyone still feel as angry as when you started? Why or why not?**

Say: **These exercises help us get rid of our anger without hurting anyone or anything. God gives us the ability to control our anger!**

CLOSING

Have kids get with their partners again. Have them each tell their partner which anger exercise they'll use the next time they're angry.

Have partners hold hands for a prayer. Pray: **Dear God, thanks for giving us the ability to handle our anger without hurting others. Amen.**

WHO'S TIED UP?

- ● **THEME:** Lies
- ● **SCRIPTURE:** John 8:31-36
- ● **OVERVIEW:** Children are wrapped up in "red and white lies" and determine which is worse.
- ● **PREPARATION:** You'll need a Bible and two rolls of crepe paper streamers (one white and one red).

EXPERIENCE

Choose two volunteers. Ask one child to hold the end of the white crepe paper roll. Have the other child hold the end of the red crepe paper roll.

Say: **One at a time, we'll tell a lie. Then we all will vote on whether it's a harmless "white lie" or an ugly "red lie." A white lie could be saying your mom won't let you play with someone when it's really you who doesn't want to play. A red lie could be lying to your parents about stealing money.**

Begin the game. Ask one person to tell a lie. Take a vote. Depending on the vote, wrap the crepe paper around one of the volunteers. Continue telling lies and voting until both volunteers are significantly bound by the crepe paper.

Then ask: **Which is worse—white lies or red lies? Explain. What does this tell us about lies—are they ever okay? How are we set free from sin?**

Say: **Both of our volunteers were tied up by sin. It didn't matter whether the lies were white or red. Let's hear what the Bible says about lies.**

RESPONSE

Read aloud John 8:31-36. Have kids each take turns ripping the crepe paper away from the volunteers, saying, "Jesus will set you free!"

Say: **Lies tie us up, but Christ's forgiveness rips through all lies and sets us free if we ask for forgiveness.**

CLOSING

Have each person hold a red or white piece of crepe paper and stand in a circle. Pray: **Lord, help us to shake off the temptation to lie about little things.** (Pause and have kids shake their crepe paper.) **Help us give all our sins and lies to you.** (Have kids throw the crepe paper in the air.) **Thanks for your forgiveness. Amen.**

23 HOW DO YOU SPELL SUCCESS?

● **THEME:** Success

● **SCRIPTURE:** Joshua 1:7-8

● **OVERVIEW:** Children create posters that define success, then compare their definitions to the Bible's definition of success.

● **PREPARATION:** You'll need a Bible, poster board, magazines, glue, tape, scissors, and markers.

EXPERIENCE

Have kids gather in a tight circle, close their eyes, and reach out with one hand to grasp one other hand. Then have them open their eyes to see whose hand they have. That person is their partner for this activity.

Say: **Together with your partner, use the supplies I've provided to make a poster that shows what success means. Make sure your poster is easy to understand, because we'll be posting them around the room. You have six minutes to complete your poster.** Kids could cut out magazine pictures of big houses, shiny cars, high-rise buildings, and beautiful clothes, then glue them to the poster board. They could also draw crowns, stars, and dollar signs.

Have each pair display, explain, and then tape their poster to a wall.

REFLECTION

Ask: **Which pair was most successful at making a success poster? Explain. How do you tell who is and isn't successful in this activity? in life? Do you agree or disagree with these pictures of success? Explain.**

Read aloud Joshua 1: 7-8. Ask: **How does the Bible say we can find success in life? How is that picture of success like or unlike the pictures on our posters? What are ways people "obey the teachings" of the Bible in everyday life? Based on what we read in the Bible, how can we be successful in life?**

CLOSING

Have pairs design a new poster that defines success the way the Bible defines it. Kids could cut out and glue pictures of church buildings, missionaries, or families laughing together and reading Bibles and books.

Then have pairs each display, explain, and tape their poster on top of their first success poster. As each pair tapes its new poster on the wall, have the rest of the kids yell, "O-B-E-Y! That's the way God spells success!"

HOMEWORK BLUES

- **THEME:** Homework
- **SCRIPTURE:** 2 Timothy 2:15
- **OVERVIEW:** Children walk across a 2×4 beam and learn about the importance of practice.
- **PREPARATION:** For each person, you'll need a piece of candy. You'll also need a Bible and a 12-foot 2×4 beam.

EXPERIENCE

Place the 2×4 beam in the middle of the room. Tell kids to take turns walking the length of the beam without falling off. Don't let them practice—just have them line up and take turns attempting to walk the beam.

If some kids are successful the first time, increase the difficulty by having them walk backward across the beam or jump on one foot. Or you could place a short block under the middle of the long beam to create a teeter-totter. Have kids walk across the teeter-totter without falling off.

RESPONSE

Have kids sit on the beam. Ask: **What was easy or hard about walking the beam? How did you feel if you weren't able to do it? What would have helped you walk the beam better? How does practice improve our skills? How is doing homework like practicing a skill?**

Read aloud 2 Timothy 2:15. Ask: **What advice does this passage give us about practice and studying hard?**

Say: **God wants us to study so we can do our best for him. After all, God created everything, and the more we learn and study about ourselves and our world, the more we learn about God. All of you could have been more successful on the beam if you had been able to practice, just like you could be even more successful at school if you do your homework. Everyone can do better if they study and practice.**

CLOSING

Have kids stand on the beam and hold hands. Pray: **Dear God, thank you for letting us be successful through practice and study. Let the beam under our feet remind us to do our best for you. Amen.**

One at a time, have kids jump off the beam and shout, "Practice! Do your homework!"

OUT OF NOTHING

● **THEME:** Insecurity, fear

● **SCRIPTURE:** Genesis 1:2; Genesis 1:31; and Philippians 4:13

● **OVERVIEW:** Children reach inside an empty box to "feel" what God used to create the world.

● **PREPARATION:** You'll need a Bible and a large empty box with a hole cut in the side.

EXPERIENCE

Have kids sit in a circle. Pass the box around and have each child reach in and feel what's inside.

Say: **Think about what you could create with what you feel in the box. As it's being passed around, keep the box's contents a secret.**

When everyone has had a chance to feel inside, ask: **What did you feel as you reached in the box? What could you create with nothing? What did God create out of nothing?**

Read aloud Genesis 1:2. Say: **Out of the same thing we felt in the box, God created everything we have ever seen.**

RESPONSE

Say: **Sometimes when we face new or unknown things, we feel insecure and scared. But God feels good about who we are and can help us to not be afraid.**

Read aloud Genesis 1:31. Say: **God felt good about everything he had created, and that includes you and me! When we feel scared about facing new situations, we can remember that God loves us and feels good about his creation. With God, we can face any new situation without fear.**

CLOSING

Read aloud Philippians 4:13. Have the kids reach out so that they feel nothingness with their hands. Pray: **Lord, we thank you for creating from nothing everything we have ever seen. When** we face new situations, help us remember that you feel good about us. With you, we can do all things. Amen.

Have kids shake hands with each other, grabbing hold of something solid and good that God created.

 # FOILED AGAIN

● **THEME:** Disappointment
● **SCRIPTURE:** Psalm 22:3-5; Matthew 20:1-16
● **OVERVIEW:** Children receive a foil-wrapped treat and learn how to view disappointments.
● **PREPARATION:** For each person, you'll need a real treat (such as a piece of candy or fruit) and a fake treat (wrap a wad of paper in aluminum foil and tie it with ribbon).

EXPERIENCE

Have children sit in a circle. Give one foil-wrapped fake treat to each child. Have kids wait to open the treats until everyone has one. When you finish handing them out, say: **Now you may open your treat.**

When children discover there's nothing inside except a wad of paper, ask: **What were you expecting? How did you feel when you didn't receive what you expected?**

RESPONSE

Say: **Let's hear about some workers who were expecting more than they received.**

Read aloud Matthew 20:1-16. Ask: **Why were the workers disappointed? Besides getting the fake treat, what other times have you been disappointed? What gift do we know waits for every**

Christian? How can knowing about God's forgiveness and gift of eternal life help you when you feel disappointed?

CLOSING

Read aloud Psalm 22:3-5. Ask: **What does this passage promise us?** Give each person a real treat and say: **When we trust God, we won't be disappointed.**

RACING WITH THE EGGS OF UNFORGIVENESS

● **THEME:** Unforgiveness

● **SCRIPTURE:** Matthew 18:21-35

● **OVERVIEW:** Children balance a plastic egg on an upside down cookie sheet and learn about unforgiveness.

● **PREPARATION:** For each person, you'll need a slip of paper and a pencil. You'll also need a Bible, one basket, two cookie sheets, and several plastic eggs (purchase these at hobby shops or discount stores).

EXPERIENCE

Form two teams. Have teams line up on one side of the room. Give the first person on each team an upside-down cookie sheet and a plastic egg. Say: **The object of the game is for you to run to the opposite side of the room and back while balancing the egg on your upside-down cookie sheet. If you drop the egg, pick it up, take one step backward, then continue. Tag the next person on your team, who repeats the process. The first team to complete the relay wins. Ready? Go!**

RESPONSE

After the race, have kids sit in a circle. Ask: **How did you feel running this race? What was easy or hard about it? How is balancing an egg like not forgiving someone?**

Say: **"Unforgiveness," or holding on to grudges, is like balancing eggs. Unforgiveness demands all your attention and slows you down.**

Read aloud Matthew 18:21-35. Ask: **What does Jesus tell us about forgiveness? How can we forgive others "from our hearts"?**

CLOSING

In the center of the circle, place a basket filled with several plastic eggs. Give each person a slip of paper and a pencil. Ask kids to write names of people with whom they're angry. Next, have kids place their slips inside the plastic eggs arranged in the basket.

Have kids join hands. Pray: **Lord, help us leave our grudges in this basket. Fill our hearts with forgiveness. Thanks for your love and forgiveness. Amen.**

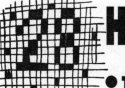 # HOW RED IS MY FACE?

● **THEME:** Embarrassment

● **SCRIPTURE:** Luke 19:1-6

● **OVERVIEW:** Children experience what it's like to feel the first pangs of embarrassment and learn that embarrassment isn't always bad. (Best for upper-elementary kids.)

● **PREPARATION:** For each person, you'll need paper, a pencil, and an envelope. You'll also need a Bible. Place a blank sheet of paper inside an envelope, seal it, and address it to yourself.

EXPERIENCE

Gather kids around you and hold up a sealed envelope addressed to you. Say: **You won't believe what's in this letter! What would you think if I told you that one of your parents decided to write me a letter about something really goofy you did last week. I mean, one of you did something REALLY embarrassing. Would you believe your parent sent this letter to me? Do you think I should open this envelope and read the letter aloud to everyone?**

Ask kids to vote on whether or not you should open the letter and read it aloud. Explain that you'll read it only if the majority votes for you to do it.

No matter how kids vote, say: **If you didn't believe your parent would send me a letter about something embarrassing you did, you were right!** (Open the envelope and show the blank paper.) **The paper is blank! I apologize for pretending it was sent by a parent.**

RESPONSE

Ask: **How did you feel when I told you I might tell the group some embarrassing secret you have? How did you feel when I told you there was nothing on the paper? When have you felt embarrassed? Was it a good or bad experience? Explain.**

Say: **Let's read about a person probably was embarrassed in front of many people, including Jesus.**

Read aloud Luke 19:1-6. Ask: **If you had been there, would you have done what Zacchaeus did? Why or why not? Do you think Zacchaeus felt it was worth the embarrassment for him to climb the tree to see Jesus? Why or why not? When is it okay to be embarrassed?**

CLOSING

Give each person a sheet of paper, a pencil, and an envelope. Ask kids to each write Jesus a letter, telling him they're not embarrassed to let others know they love him. Have them each place their letter in their envelope, seal it, and take it home for safekeeping. Ask them to keep it until their next birthday, then read it aloud for their family or friends.

WHERE'S THE TARGET?

● **THEME:** Goals

● **SCRIPTURE:** Philippians 3:14

● **OVERVIEW:** Children play darts with no target and learn what living life without goals is like. (Best for upper-elementary kids.)

● **PREPARATION:** For each person, you'll need a pencil and a photocopy of the "Taking Aim" handout (p. 50). You'll also need a Bible, tape, and a toy dart set with a target (borrow a set from a child in your church or purchase one at a discount store).

EXPERIENCE

Hand the darts to several children (don't bring out the target yet). Challenge kids to see who's the best at darts. When one person asks about the target, bring out the target and tape it to a wall. Have all kids take turns throwing darts at the target.

RESPONSE

Collect the darts, then have kids sit down in a circle. Ask: **What difference does a target make in a game? How is throwing darts at a target like aiming for goals in life?**

Say: **When you throw at a target, you know what to aim for. You have a set goal. With no target or no goals, you can't play the game. Life is like that, too.**

Read aloud Philippians 3:14. Ask: **What are goals you can have for school?** (For example, "get good grades" or "listen to teachers.") **What are goals you can have for your faith?** (For example, "learning more about Jesus" or "bringing a friend to Sunday school.") **What are goals you have for your family?** (For example, "get along with my sister" or "obey my parents.")

Give each person a "Taking Aim" handout and a pencil. Encourage kids to each write a school goal and a faith goal on the target.

CLOSING

Have kids read their goals aloud and tape their handouts around the real target. Read aloud Philippians 3:14. Then, have kids join hands as you pray: **Lord, help us aim for our school goals and learn all we can. Help us aim for our faith goals and grow closer to you. Help us aim for our family goals and grow closer to our families. Please guide us each day of our lives. Amen.**

Leave the handouts taped around the target as a reminder to aim for goals.

TAKING AIM

Write one school goal in the center of the target; for example, "get better grades" or "listen to my teacher." Write one faith goal in the center of the target; for example, "learn more about Jesus" or "bring a friend to Sunday school." Then write one family goal in the center of the target, for example, "get along better with my sister" or "help my mom with the dishes."

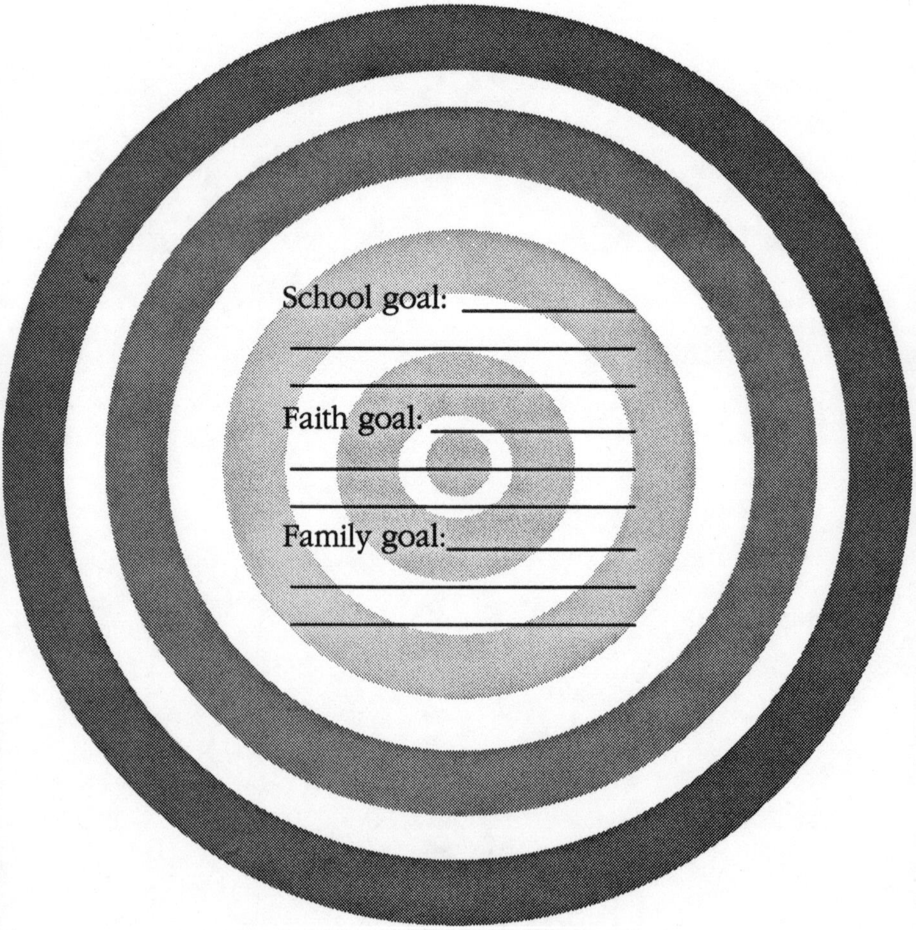

School goal: _____

_____

_____

Faith goal: _____

_____

_____

Family goal: _____

_____

_____

ALL ALONE

● **THEME:** Loneliness

● **SCRIPTURE:** Matthew 28:20b

● **OVERVIEW:** Children experience being alone, then talk with a partner about how God is always near.

● **PREPARATION:** For each person, you'll need a sheet of paper and a pencil. You'll also need a Bible.

EXPERIENCE

Say: **We're going to experience being alone. Everyone spread out in the room so you can't talk to each other. Then close your eyes so you can't see each other. Stay this way for two minutes.**

After two minutes, have kids each find a partner. Say: **After this alone time, I want you to talk to your partner about when you've felt alone and when you've felt God's nearness.**

Give kids two minutes to talk.

RESPONSE

After two minutes, have kids sit in a circle. Ask: **How did you feel when you were by yourself? How did you feel when you were talking with a friend? When did time go faster—when you were alone or when you were talking with a friend? How is the way you felt when talking to a friend like the way you feel when you know God is near? How can Jesus comfort you when you feel lonely?**

Read aloud Matthew 28:20b. Say: **Jesus promises to always be with us. We can pray to him at any time or in any place. He is always there.**

CLOSING

Have kids silently pray, thanking God for being near. Then pray aloud: **Thank you, God, for promising to always be with us. You are as near to us as the friend we're sitting next to.**

Whenever we're lonely, help us remember you're right by our side. Amen.

CHEATER! CHEATER!

- ● **THEME:** Cheating
- ● **SCRIPTURE:** Acts 5:1-10
- ● **OVERVIEW:** Children experience the temptation to cheat.
- ● **PREPARATION:** For each person, you'll need a candy bar. You'll also need a Bible, two sheets of paper, and two pencils.

EXPERIENCE

Form two groups. Have groups each form a circle on the floor 3 feet from each other. Give each group a sheet of paper and a pencil. Say: **You have two minutes to think of 10 things that show people are honest; for example, "honest people don't cheat." Choose someone to write the ideas on your paper. Work in your own group and don't look at other group's papers. The group with the most ideas listed will win a prize.**

RESPONSE

After two minutes, ask one person from each group to read the list. Award candy bars to the group with the most ideas listed.

Ask: **How easy or difficult was it to work in your own group? Were you tempted to listen to the other group? Why or why not? How was this activity like or unlike real-life situations where it's tempting to cheat?**

Say: **Let's read in the Bible about two people who cheated.**

Give everyone a candy bar. Have kids eat their goodies and listen as you read aloud Acts 5:1-10. Ask: **Why is honesty important to God?**

CLOSING

Have kids form a circle and hold hands. Have the person to your left pray silently about his or her desire to be honest. When that person is finished praying, he or she squeezes the hand of the person to the left. Continue until your hand is squeezed and say "Amen."

HIDING BEHIND MASKS

- **THEME:** Being yourself
- **SCRIPTURE:** Psalm 139:1-6
- **OVERVIEW:** Children make masks and learn that God loves them just the way they are.
- **PREPARATION:** For each person, you'll need markers, scissors, and a paper grocery sack. You'll also need a Bible.

EXPERIENCE

Give each person markers, scissors, and a paper grocery sack. Have kids cut eye holes in their sacks, then decorate the sacks. Ask kids to put on their masks. Give them two minutes to greet as many people as they can saying, "Hi! Do you know who I am?" Have kids keep track of how many people know them even with their masks on.

RESPONSE

After two minutes, have kids sit in a circle and take off their masks. Ask: **How many people knew who you were, even though you were wearing a mask? When in real life have you "worn a mask" and pretended to be different than you really are? Does God see behind our masks? Why do we hide behind masks in real life? Why is it hard to be ourselves when we're in a new situation or when we're with people we don't know?**

Say: **Let's see what the Bible says about hiding who we are or what we do from God.**

Read aloud Psalm 139:1-6. Ask: **Can we pretend to be what we're not with God? Why or why not? What does God think about the "real you"?**

CLOSING

Have kids write on their masks "God knows all about me—and God loves me."

Ask kids to each take home their mask and hang it by a bedroom or bathroom mirror. Each time kids look in the mirror, have them look at the mask and remember to be themselves—God loves them just the way they are.

GRADE ANXIETY

● **THEME:** Grades

● **SCRIPTURE:** 1 Corinthians 9:24-25

● **OVERVIEW:** Children are given different motivations for winning a relay race. (Best for upper-elementary kids.)

● **PREPARATION:** You'll need a Bible and prizes, such as fruit slices or cans of juice.

EXPERIENCE

Say: **We're going to run a fun relay race. But first, let's work together to design an obstacle course in our meeting room.** Ask kids to use materials in your room for the obstacle course and to pick a start-and-finish line. For example, kids could arrange tables to crawl under, chairs to run around, and wastebaskets to hop over.

After a few minutes, gather kids together and form two equal-number teams, the Olympians and the Superstars. Huddle with the Olympians and quietly tell them that if they win the race, they'll earn a prize. Then huddle with the Superstars and quietly tell them they're running the race just for pride or knowing they did their best.

Tell both teams to line up single file at the start-and-finish line. On "go," the first person in each line should run the obstacle course, then tag the next person in line, and so on. The first team to have all its members finish the obstacle course, wins.

If the Olympians win, give each team member a prize. If the Superstars win, declare them the winners, but don't give them a prize. Applaud both teams for their efforts.

RESPONSE

Have kids sit in a circle, then tell them what you told each team before the race.

Ask: **Olympians, did you try harder to win because I promised you a prize? Why or why not? Superstars, why did you try hard to win if there was no prize waiting for you at the end? How are grades like or unlike prizes? What's more important—getting good grades or trying your hardest? Explain.**

CLOSING

Give everyone a prize, then ask kids to listen as you read aloud 1 Corinthians 9:24-25. Ask: **According to this passage, what's more important—winning or trying hard? Explain. What's more important than getting good grades? Explain.**

Turn off the lights and say: **Grades can encourage us to do our best, and they can cause us to worry. Let's go around the circle and pray for each other's grade worries.**

Ask each person to call out one grade worry (a class or a test), then have the group respond, "Lord, help us run the race" after each person shares.

FOOT SNARES

● **THEME:** Confidence

● **SCRIPTURE:** Proverbs 3:23-26

● **OVERVIEW:** Children walk around a "trap" and learn to trust God to give them confidence.

● **PREPARATION:** You'll need a Bible, a blanket, a card table, tape, and eight sheets of paper. Write one of these words on a separate sheet of paper: fear, tiredness, danger, confusion, courage, strength, safety, and understanding.

EXPERIENCE

Place the card table in the middle of the room. Gather kids around it. Cover the table with a blanket and say: **Sometimes we are covered with things that take away our confidence.** Have kids read each of these four signs as you tape one to each side of the table: fear, tiredness, danger, and confusion.

Ask: **Have you ever been afraid to try something new, such as riding a roller coaster or going to a new school? Why or why not? What are reasons we don't feel good about doing some things?**

Say: **Sometimes our fears and other feelings take away our confidence. They trap us and keep us from trying new things. Let's see what it's like to be trapped by our fears.**

Ask a volunteer to sit under the table and be the "trapper." The trapper's job is to grab other kids' feet as they walk around the table. Tell the trapper to let go as soon as he or she grabs a foot, so nobody gets hurt.

Have the other children walk around the table, jumping away only when the trapper tries to grab them. Have kids read each sign as they walk past it.

Let kids take turns hiding under the table and trapping others.

RESPONSE

Gather everyone, including the trapper, in a circle around the table. Say a prayer as you take off an old sign and replace it with a new sign as follows: **God we ask you to replace our fear with courage; our tiredness with strength; our feelings of danger with feelings of safety; our confusion with understanding. Thanks for these gifts to help us feel confident.**

Have kids walk around the table and listen as you read aloud Proverbs 3:23-26.

Have kids stop and sit in a circle around the table. Ask: **Who gives us confidence and helps us to do hard or scary things? How can God make us more confident?**

CLOSING

Say: **These four new signs on the table are good reminders of ways God can help us to not be afraid.**

Have kids hold hands. Pray: **Dear God, we need you to give us confidence every day. Thanks for being so big and strong that no matter what happens, you can help us not to be afraid. Amen.**

WHAT TO DO ABOUT SCHOOL

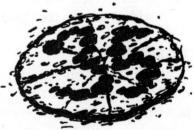

● **THEME:** School worries

● **SCRIPTURE:** Psalm 139:23

● **OVERVIEW:** Children experience the anxiety of facing a test and the peace that comes through prayer.

● **PREPARATION:** For each person, you'll need a brand-new pencil. You'll also need a Bible and several sheets of paper.

EXPERIENCE

Tell kids to find a place in the room where they'll be able to work quietly. Choose a subject that your group has recently talked about and tell kids that in a minute you'll test them on that subject.

(Of course, you won't really test the kids, but let them think you're going to. Look busy by gathering pencils and shuffling papers.)

After a minute, ask kids to get quiet and remind them not to talk, because this a test. When everyone is quiet, say: **Close your eyes and think about Jesus for the next 20 seconds. Ask Jesus to help you do well on the test.**

After 20 seconds, pray aloud: **God, help these children do well on the test. Give them peace inside to do their best. Amen.**

After you finish praying, say: **Before you take the test, I want to ask you some questions.**

RESPONSE

Ask: **When I announced you were going to take a test, did you feel worried or peaceful? Explain. After we prayed, did you feel worried or peaceful? Explain. How can a silent prayer help you at school when you have to take a test or other times you feel worried or nervous?**

Read aloud Psalm 139:23. Say: **I have good news: God knows when we are worried or nervous. God can replace our worries with peace when we ask him to. And here's more good news: I've decided not to test you after all.**

CLOSING

Give each person a brand-new pencil. Tell kids they can keep the pencils as reminders to pray to Jesus when they feel worried or nervous in school or anywhere else.

Have kids hold their pencils and stand in a circle. Ask them to say "thanks" each time you pause during the prayer.

Pray: **Thanks for Jesus and the following gifts you've given us: for being with us at all times and in all places when we feel worried or nervous;** (pause) **for giving us peace when we feel worried or nervous at school, home, church, or anywhere else;** (pause) **for always being as close to us as the pencil we're holding;** (pause) **for being even more faithful and helpful to us during a test than this pencil;** (pause) **and especially for your forgiveness and love.** (pause) **Amen.**

A LOT OF HOT AIR

● **THEME:** Bragging
● **SCRIPTURE:** Jeremiah 9:24
● **OVERVIEW:** Children experience the futility of bragging about themselves and the importance of giving God the credit.
● **PREPARATION:** For each person, you'll need a jar of bubbles (available at grocery or discount stores). You'll also need a Bible.

EXPERIENCE

Give each child a jar of bubbles. Give kids three minutes to blow bubbles as they brag about things they've done this week; for example, "I rode my bike five miles," "I got an A on my test," or "I can draw better than my brother."

After three minutes, say "stop." Watch all the soap bubbles disappear and pop. Have kids bring their jar of bubbles and sit in a circle.

RESPONSE

Ask: **What happened to all your bubbles? How are the popping, disappearing bubbles like bragging about ourselves?**

Say: **Those bubbles were filled with all the great things we've done all week. When we brag about ourselves, our boasts pop and disappear. Listen to what the Bible says about bragging.**

Read aloud Jeremiah 9:24.

Say: **Think about those same things you bragged about earlier, only this time, hold up your jar of bubbles and shout, "Not I, but the Lord in me!"**

Have kids hold up their jars and shout. Then say: **Look at your jar of bubbles and see what you've got to play with! When we boast in the Lord, we have something to hang on to and feel good about!**

CLOSING

As a closing prayer, go around the circle and have kids brag about

God; for example, "God can make anything," "With God, I can do anything," or "God is wonderful."

Let kids each take home their jar of bubbles as reminders to hang on to and tell others about God.

37 PUZZLING PEOPLE

● **THEME:** Self-worth
● **SCRIPTURE:** Jeremiah 29:11
● **OVERVIEW:** Children play with puzzles and learn that everyone has a place in God's ultimate plan.
● **PREPARATION:** You'll need a Bible and prizes, such as stickers or candy. For every three to four children, you'll need one age-appropriate puzzle. Place the pieces for each puzzle in separate piles at various spots around the room. Take one piece from each pile and place it in one of the other piles.

EXPERIENCE

Gather the children and ask: **Have you ever felt lonely or seen someone who was all alone? How do you feel when other children are playing together and you're left out?**

Say: **God created everyone with a purpose. And we each have a place to fit in God's plan.**

Read aloud Jeremiah 29:11.

Form groups of three or four. Ask each group to find a puzzle and put it together. Say: **The first group to complete its puzzle gets a prize.** When kids comment about the "misfit" piece in their piles, say: **Even though that piece may not seem valuable to you, it's very important to the completion of another group's puzzle.**

Have kids figure out who gets the "misfit" pieces. When the puzzles are completed, ask kids to sit in a circle.

RESPONSE

Ask: **What was easy or hard about this activity? How did you feel as you were figuring out who needed your "misfit" puzzle piece? How did you feel finding your own missing piece? How is this activity like knowing we each have a purpose and we each are special?**

Say: **God loves each one of us and has plans for us.**

CLOSING

Give each child a prize and say: **You're a winner in God's eyes.** Ask: **Since every person is important in God's plan, how should we treat everyone—especially people who don't seem to fit in or seem to be lonely?**

Close by praying: **Dear God, help us remember that everyone is important in your eyes. Help us treat everyone with kindness. Thanks for loving each of us equally. Thanks for your plan for our lives. Thanks for hope and our good futures. Amen.**

A REAL SUCCESS

● **THEME:** Success

● **SCRIPTURE:** Psalm 1:1-3

● **OVERVIEW:** Children blow cotton balls into a cup and learn the true meaning of success.

● **PREPARATION:** For each person, you'll need a pencil and a bookmark-sized piece of poster board. You'll also need cotton balls, paper cups, and a Bible.

EXPERIENCE

Form trios. Give each trio several cotton balls and a paper cup. Have trio members place their cotton balls on the floor, 3 feet away from their cup. Then have them work together to blow the cotton balls into their cup.

RESPONSE

After each trio has successfully completed the task, have everyone sit in a circle. Ask: **How did you feel when you succeeded in the game? How do you feel when you succeed in something at school? What does it take to be a success?**

Say: **God wants us to be successful. Let's listen to what the Bible says about success.**

Read aloud Psalm 1:1-3. Ask: **What does this passage tell us to do to be successful? How does "thinking about God's teachings" help us succeed in life?**

CLOSING

Give each person a pencil and a bookmark-sized piece of poster board. Say: **Think of one thing you can do to spend more time reading the Bible. For example, you could read one chapter in the Bible daily, or you could read the Bible right before you go to bed. Write your idea on this bookmark.**

After kids finish, take turns reading the ideas. Then say: **Take your bookmark home and place it in your Bible as a reminder to "love the Lord's teachings."**

PROMISES, PROMISES

- ● **THEME:** Keeping promises
- ● **SCRIPTURE:** James 5:12
- ● **OVERVIEW:** Children challenge each other to run a relay race and experience how hard it is to keep unreal promises.
- ● **PREPARATION:** You'll need a Bible, a bucket of water, a spoon, a small glass, and prizes, such as cans of soft drinks.

EXPERIENCE

Form two teams and play Name That Promise! Set a bucket of water at one end of the room. Then set a small, empty glass and a spoon at the other end of the room. Have teams each line up single file on either side of the glass, facing the bucket at the other end of the room.

Say: **The goal of this game is to use the spoon to fill up the empty glass with water. One by one, each person on your team must run with the spoon down to the bucket, fill it with water, carefully bring it back, and dump the water into the glass, then pass the spoon to the next person in line. You'll keep doing this until the glass is full.**

Say: **Here's the catch—only one team can attempt this feat. As a team, you must decide how quickly you can fill up the glass. Each team will take turns promising how fast they can fill up the glass. For example, Team 1 might say, "We can fill that glass in four minutes," and Team 2 might respond "We can fill that glass in three minutes." Your team should keep promising a faster time until you think the other team can't do it in the time they've promised. If that happens, call out, "Keep your promise!" Then the other team will try to fill the glass in the time they've promised. If they do it, they win a prize. If they don't, your team wins the prize.**

Tell teams to start promising faster and faster times. When one team forces the other to keep its promise, time that team to see if it can do it. Award the winning team members each a soft drink.

RESPONSE

Ask: **How did you feel when you promised something you weren't sure you could do? How did you feel when you kept or didn't keep that promise? How is that like the way you feel when you keep or don't keep promises in real life? What makes it hard to keep promises? What makes it easy? Why is it important to keep our promises?**

CLOSING

Give everyone a soft drink and have them listen as you read aloud James 5:12. Say: **Think of one thing you can promise God** with a solid "yes," such as "being nice to my little brother" or "bringing a friend to church." When I call out, "God, I promise you that I'll..." all of us will yell out our promise at the same time. Ready? God, I promise you that I'll...

Section 3:
FUN DEVOTIONS ABOUT OTHERS

LOOKING FOR GOOD IN ALL THE RIGHT PLACES

● **THEME:** Seeing good in others

● **SCRIPTURE:** 1 Samuel 16:1-12

● **OVERVIEW:** Children go on a treasure hunt and learn that they have to look below the surface to find "treasure." (Best for upper-elementary kids.)

● **PREPARATION:** You'll need a Bible, paper, markers, and tape. Ask your kids to bring a small "treasure" from home (such as a ring, toy, favorite pen, or book) to the meeting.

EXPERIENCE

As kids arrive, ask them to give you their small treasures from home. If some kids forget to bring a treasure, give them paper and markers and ask them to quickly draw a treasure from home and give you the drawing.

Then say: **Today we're going to play Hide-and-Seek. But I'll do the hiding, and you'll do the seeking!**

Have kids huddle together in a corner of your room facing the wall. Ask them to close their eyes and slowly count to 100 together. While they're counting, quickly hide their treasures in the room. When kids reach 100, tell them to open their eyes.

Say: **Find a partner standing close to you.** (pause) **While you've been counting, I've been hiding your treasures in this room. Your mission is to seek and find your treasure. But there's a catch. Only your partner is allowed to find *your* treasure. Quickly describe your treasure to your partner, then search to find what your partner has described. If you see your treasure as you're looking for your partner's, leave it where it's hidden and don't say anything. Only your partner can find your treasure for you. Ready? Go!**

RESPONSE

After kids have each retrieved their partner's treasure, ask them to sit with their partner and tell why the treasure they brought with them is important.

Ask: **How did you feel as you were looking for your partner's treasure? How did you feel when your partner found your treasure? What did you learn about your partner from the kind of treasure he or she brought? What's one great thing about your partner that most people don't know? How is looking for others' treasures like seeing the good in other people?**

Read aloud 1 Samuel 16:1-12. Then ask: **What did God see in David that others didn't? Why does God see good in us when others don't? How can we learn to see the good in other people?**

CLOSING

Give each person a sheet of paper and a marker. Have kids each write one "hidden treasure" about their partner, such as "Jacob cares for other people" or "Karen is patient. She doesn't get mad easily." Younger kids might simply draw a picture for their partners.

Then gather in a circle. Ask kids to each read aloud what they've written about their partner, then give the paper to their partner. Close by getting in a tight huddle. Have kids each look at the person across from them. Together, yell, "I see the good in you!"

WHO WINS?

● **THEME:** Competition

● **SCRIPTURE:** Colossians 3:23

● **OVERVIEW:** Children play a ball game and learn about doing their best and persevering.

● **PREPARATION:** For each person, you'll need an inexpensive ball. You'll also need a Bible.

EXPERIENCE

Form pairs and give each pair a ball. Say: **The object of this game is to keep the ball moving between you and your part-**

ner. As soon as one of you drops the ball, you both have to sit down. Ready? Go!

If kids ask for more instructions say: **Just keep the ball moving!** Notice the different ways kids try to accomplish the objective. Some may throw hard and take big risks. Some may bat the ball back and forth and burn out quickly. Some may become angry because their partner missed and got them "out." Some may "beat the system" by gently handing the ball back and forth.

RESPONSE

Tell kids to hold the balls and sit down. Read aloud Colossians 3:23. Ask: **How did you feel about trying to win this game? What did you notice about the different ways pairs kept their balls moving? How is our ball game like our race to heaven?**

Say: **The pairs who kept the ball moving the longest did so by passing it back and forth slowly and carefully. The Bible says we are always to do our best. It doesn't say "so you can win" or "so people will say you're the best." It says to do it for the Lord. We don't win by throwing the hardest, being the fastest, breaking the rules, or quitting. We win when we do our best for God.**

CLOSING

Reread Colossians 3:23 so kids can hear again God's principles of winning. Have partners face each other. As you say the following prayer, have kids hand their ball to their partner—back and forth, slowly and surely.

Pray: **Thank you, Lord, for allowing us to have fun in this game. Help us remember that your ideas about what makes a winner are most important. Help us realize that when we do our best for your sake, we are winners. Amen.**

Give kids each a ball and tell them to remember to do their best.

HOWDY NEIGHBOR

● **THEME:** Making friends
● **SCRIPTURE:** Hebrews 10:24-25
● **OVERVIEW:** Children memorize names and learn about making friends.
● **PREPARATION:** For every person, you'll need a chair. You'll also need a Bible.

EXPERIENCE

As kids enter the room, ask them to find a chair, place it in a circle, and sit down. Say: **Today we're going to learn two important parts of making friends: learning their names and finding out how they feel. First, let's go around the circle and we'll say our names. Try to remember everyone's name, because names will be important in our game.**

After everyone has said his or her name, say: **Now, let's practice showing different feelings. Everyone show me how you look when you're sad,** (pause) **happy** (pause).

Ask one child to stand in the middle of the circle. Remove his or her chair from the circle. Explain the rules:

● **The center person must point to any seated player and ask, "How's your neighbor?" and slowly start counting to 10.**

● **The "neighbors" sitting on either side of the seated person make a "happy" or "sad" face.**

● **The person being pointed to then must say, "*(Name of a neighbor)* is happy" or "*(Name of a neighbor)* is sad," depending on the neighbor's facial expression.**

● **If the person being pointed to responds, "*(Name)* is happy" before the center person has counted to 10, the center person remains standing and points to another person.**

● **If the person being pointed to responds with the wrong name or does not respond within 10 seconds, the seated person and the center person must trade places.**

● **If the person being pointed to responds with "*(Name)* is sad," then everyone in the circle must jump up and find a new** seat. **The center person must also try to find a seat. Whoever is left standing is the new center person.**

Remind the more competitive players to be gentle when trying to find a new seat.

RESPONSE

Add the extra chair so everyone can sit in the circle. Ask: **How easy or hard was it to remember names? to recognize feelings? How easy or hard is it to do these things in real life?**

Read aloud Hebrews 10:24-25. Ask: **What does this passage say we should do when we meet together? How does knowing someone's name help us make friends? How does knowing someone's feelings help us make friends?**

CLOSING

Go around the circle. Have each person complete this sentence for the person on his or her right: "You are a good friend because..." For example, kids might say, "because you're good at remembering names," "because you always ask how I'm feeling," or "because you make me happy when I'm sad."

After everyone is affirmed, pray: **Dear Lord, help us be good friends. Thank you for Jesus, our best friend of all. Amen.**

WE CAN WORK IT OUT

● **THEME:** Family conflicts

● **SCRIPTURE:** Hebrews 12:14

● **OVERVIEW:** Children compete in a Tug of War that neither team wins unless they cooperate. (Best for upper-elementary kids.)

● **PREPARATION:** You'll need a Bible, a bag of

goodies, 20 feet of thread, scissors, newsprint, a marker, and masking tape.

EXPERIENCE

Form two teams for Tug of War. Clear the middle of your meeting room to make room for the competition. Place a piece of masking tape on the floor as a divider between the teams. Then lay 20 feet of thread on the floor in a straight line, with 10 feet of thread on either side of the masking tape.

Say: **The object of this Tug of War is for each team to pull on its end of the thread and drag everyone on the other team across the masking tape line. If your team is successful, you win a bag of goodies. But listen carefully: If the thread breaks, neither team wins anything! So, think about the best way to really win this competition.**

Give teams one minute to plan their strategy. Then have each team grab its end of the thread. On "go," have them start the competition.

RESPONSE

Since it's impossible for one team to really drag the other across the line without breaking the thread, the only way kids can win this Tug of War is to agree to split the winnings with the other team. One team can agree to let itself be "dragged" across the line, then the two teams can divide the goodies. If kids don't decide to do this and the thread breaks, don't award the goodies to either team.

If the thread breaks, ask: **How did you feel as your team planned its strategy? Was this an impossible Tug of War to win? Why or why not? What could your team have done differently to win the goodies? How could your teams have worked together to get at least some of the goodies?**

If teams successfully cooperate to win the goodies, ask: **How did you feel about your solution to this Tug of War? Was this the best way to compete? Why or why not?**

Read aloud Hebrews 12:14. Then ask: **How was this Tug of War like conflicts or problems you have in your family? When you face a problem with a family member, do you usually work with the person to find a solution? Why or why not? Why is it important to "live in peace" with your family? What are ways you've tried to "live in peace" with others?**

71

Write on newsprint kids' suggestions , such as "be patient," "be happy," "count to 10 when I get mad" and "talk to the person I'm mad at."

CLOSING

Place the thread and the scissors in the center of your room and have kids gather around them. Ask kids to each look at the newsprint list and choose one idea to try the next time they have a problem with a family member. One by one, have kids step forward, cut a small piece of thread, and say aloud the idea they'll try.

Have kids help each other tie their thread pieces around a finger as a reminder of their idea. Then close in prayer, asking God's help to live in peace.

YAKETY-YAK

● **THEME:** Gossip
● **SCRIPTURE:** Proverbs 11:13; 20:19
● **OVERVIEW:** Children blow flour and compare it to gossip.
● **PREPARATION:** You'll need a Bible, flour, a spoon, and a vacuum or broom.

EXPERIENCE

Say: **Today we're going to talk about gossip—telling personal or secret things about others. But first, what are some gossipy things we say? Use only imaginary names and situations!** For example, kids could say, "Did you know David flunked a test?" Or "Susan is grounded for a month." Or "Sally's parents are getting a divorce, but nobody's supposed to know."

Have children stand in a circle and each hold out their right hand, palm up. Tell them they're not to do anything until you give them instructions. Place a spoonful of flour in each palm. Then say: **The flour in your hand represents gossip. The object of this activi-**

ty is to spread your gossip. When I say "gossip," walk around the group and say gossipy things about imaginary people. Each time you hear a person gossip, say, "That's gossip." The person who was gossiping must blow some of the flour out of his or her hand. Then that person must try to pick up the flour before he or she can spread more gossip. After two minutes, I'll say, "Stop gossiping." Ready? Gossip!

Allow kids two minutes to gossip, then say: **Stop gossiping.**

RESPONSE

Have kids sit in a circle with any remaining flour in their hands. Ask: **How do you feel about how much flour or "gossip" you still have in your hand? How did you feel when another person said you were gossiping? How hard was it when you tried to pick up the flour after you blew it out of your hand? How is this activity like gossiping in everyday life?**

Read Proverbs 11:13 and 20:19. Say: **Sometimes it's hard to keep secrets, and it takes practice to have control over what we say. Just like the flour couldn't be picked up after it was blown, the words we say can't be picked up either. But the difference is that the flour didn't hurt anybody, while our words can hurt someone else deeply. God tells us to be trustworthy followers and to keep secrets. And God warns us to stay away from a person who talks too much and is a gossip.**

CLOSING

Tell kids that if they don't have any flour or "gossip" left, you'll give them a little more. Tell them that after the prayer and on the count of three, everyone will toss their flour into the air as a sign to God that they want no more gossip in their lives.

Pray: **God, thanks for telling us to keep secrets and for warning us to stay away from others who gossip. God, at the end of this prayer, we'll toss flour to you as a sign that we want no more gossip in our lives. Thanks for helping us get rid of gossip. Amen. Ready? One, two, three!**

After kids toss their flour, bring out the vacuum or broom and have kids help you clean up the mess caused by all that gossip!

INNER WORTH

● **THEME:** Judging others

● **SCRIPTURE:** 1 Kings 8:39; 1 Samuel 16:7

● **OVERVIEW:** Children examine two pens and learn not to judge others by outward appearances.

● **PREPARATION:** You'll need a Bible, two identical pens, and two sheets of paper. Remove one pen's inside parts.

EXPERIENCE

Have kids sit in a circle. Show them the two pens from a distance. Ask: **What difference can you see in the two pens?**

Next, place the two sheets of paper in front of two children. Give one of the pens to each person. Have them use their pens to write their name on the paper.

Ask: **Now what differences can you see in the two pens?**

Say: **When we saw the pens at a distance they looked the same. But as we looked more closely, we found that only one worked. Only one pen had what was important on the inside to be useful and good for writing. Let's hear what God says about our "insides."**

RESPONSE

Read aloud 1 Kings 8:39 and 1 Samuel 16:7. Ask: **What does God look at—our inside qualities or our outside appearance? Explain. What has God asked us to do about how we talk about or judge others? Is it easy or hard to look at a person's insides but not his or her outsides? Explain.**

CLOSING

Have one person sit in the center of the circle. One at a time, have kids say an "inside" quality they like about that person, such as "You're nice" or "You're friendly" rather than "You're cute" or "I love your hair." Make sure everyone has a chance to sit in the center and be affirmed.

Close with prayer, asking God to help us look past outside appearances and appreciate inside goodness.

FIGHTING THE GREEN-EYED MONSTER

● **THEME:** Jealousy

● **SCRIPTURE:** Matthew 20:20-28

● **OVERVIEW:** Children experience jealousy and learn how to be content with what they have.

● **PREPARATION:** You'll need a Bible, a bag of candy bars, and a bag of peanuts.

EXPERIENCE

Set on a table enough candy bars and peanuts for each person to have one candy bar or one peanut (you'll want about half of your kids to have a candy bar and the other half to have a peanut).

Say: **I've brought treats for everyone. Each of you gets to have either a candy bar or a peanut. Since there aren't enough candy bars to go around, you'll have to be quick to get one. When I shout, "Come and get it!" you can race to get your treat. Ready? Come and get it!**

After kids each get their treat, have them sit in a circle.

RESPONSE

Ask: **Those of you who didn't get a candy bar, how do you feel? Those of you who did get a candy bar, how do you feel? Is it fair that only half of you got a candy bar? Why or why not?**

Read aloud Matthew 20:20-28. Ask: **Why were the rest of the disciples angry with the two brothers? What does it mean to be jealous of someone? When have you felt jealous of someone? What does Jesus say we should do when we feel jealous?**

CLOSING

Pull out the bag with the rest of the candy bars in it. Ask the kids who got a candy bar to go to the bag, pull out a candy bar and give it to someone who didn't get one before. Close by asking kids to think of a person they're jealous of, then think of a way they can serve that person.

HONORED SOLDIERS

● **THEME:** Loyalty
● **SCRIPTURE:** Ephesians 6:7-8
● **OVERVIEW:** Children make medals for people who have demonstrated loyalty in God's army.
● **PREPARATION:** You'll need several photocopies of the "Honored Soldier" handout (p. 78). You'll also need a Bible, scissors, markers, star stickers, glitter, and glue.

EXPERIENCE

Welcome kids and have them sit in a circle. Ask: **Have you ever seen someone get a medal? What is a medal's purpose? Why is a medal a good way to honor and thank someone?**

Say: **Sometimes soldiers get special medals. Serving a country faithfully by being a good soldier is often called loyalty. People who are loyal to God faithfully serve God and others.**

Read aloud Ephesians 6:7-8. Ask kids to name people in the church who have demonstrated great sacrifice for others; for example, the pastor, the pastor's spouse, a secretary, a Sunday school teacher, or an usher.

Form small groups. Give each group an "Honored Soldier" handout, scissors, markers, stars stickers, glitter, and glue. Give each group the name of one person who has served the church. Say: **Your group is going to make a medal of honor for your assigned faithful church person. Use the supplies to decorate your medal however you want.**

RESPONSE

Have kids show their decorated medals. Ask: **What qualities do these people show in their lives that you would like to show in your lives?** Have each person say one quality, such as "fun," "loving," "loyal," or "faithful."

CLOSING

Start a prayer time by having kids name the person whose medal they designed. Close by praying: **Dear Lord, help make us faithful in everything you ask us to do, just like these loyal soldiers are faithful to you. Amen.**

Choose a time to distribute your medals. Ask the pastor for time during church announcements to call these people forward and have children pin the medals on them. Give each person a hug or a salute and lead the congregation in singing a song, such as "Onward Christian Soldiers."

HONORED SOLDIER

Decorate this medal for a person in your church who has been loyal in God's army.

WARNING SIGNALS

● **THEME:** Compassion

● **SCRIPTURE:** Luke 10:25-37

● **OVERVIEW:** Children hear different warning signals and learn about compassion.

● **PREPARATION:** You'll need any or all of the following: an alarm clock, a bicycle horn or bell, a coach's whistle, an egg timer, or any other signal you can find. You'll also need a Bible.

EXPERIENCE

Say: **I'm going to hold up and sound off different warning signals. After each one, tell me what the warning is and what you would do if you heard this signal in real life.**

Hold up and sound off the following:

● Alarm clock (Warning: It's morning—time to get up.)

● Bicycle horn or bell (Warning: A bicyclist is coming—move out of the way.)

● Coach's whistle (Warning: Foul in the game—stop and take the penalty.)

● Egg timer (Warning: Food is done—shut off the stove.)

RESPONSE

Say: **Just like these warning signals, people give signals when something is wrong.**

Ask: **What's the signal your body gives when you're hungry? tired? sad? What signals does a person sitting by himself in the lunchroom give? a person walking with her head down after an important test? How can we respond to the signals others send us? How would Jesus respond?**

Read aloud Luke 10:25-37. Ask: **What did the good Samaritan do for the person in need?**

Say: **Compassion means listening to the warning signals others send us and helping them. Sometimes we can do things for others, such as listening to our friends when they have a prob-**

lem or playing with a sister when she's lonely. Other times we can ask adults to help, such as in gathering blankets for homeless people.

CLOSING

Form small groups, enough so each group will have one warning signal. Give kids three minutes to think about one way they'll reach out and help someone who sends out a warning signal this week.

After three minutes, have small groups report their ideas to the whole group. After groups each describe the way they'll respond to a warning signal, have them sound their signal.

Have everyone hold hands. Pray: **God, help us see the signals others send us for help. Please help us lend a loving hand whenever we can. Amen.**

EVERYBODY'S IMPORTANT!

- **● THEME:** Being left out
- **● SCRIPTURE:** 1 Corinthians 12:14-25
- **● OVERVIEW:** Children depend on each other's unique abilities to complete a difficult journey.
- **● PREPARATION:** You'll need a Bible, cotton balls, blindfolds, masking tape, and string.

EXPERIENCE

Form teams of three and have each team line up single-file. Give each team some string. Have team members use the string to loosely tie their legs together. The string should have enough slack in it that each team can walk forward while tied together.

Say: **Your team must work together in your dif-**

ficult journey ahead. **Your task is to leave this room, walk outside of the building, walk all the way around the building, then return to this room. But first, you must further prepare your team members.** (You may need to adjust the course based on your building. Choose a course that will take 5 to 7 minutes.)

Give each team two blindfolds, four cotton balls, and two pieces of masking tape. In each team, have kids blindfold and put cotton in one person's ears, blindfold and put masking tape across another person's mouth, and put cotton in the ears and masking tape across the mouth of the last person.

Say: **Make sure your blindfolds, tape, and cotton balls stay in place the whole time. I'll follow along to help if you need it. Ready? Start your journey!**

RESPONSE

When teams return to your meeting room, have them remove their string, blindfolds, cotton balls, and masking tape. Ask: **How important were the other people on your team? Could you have made it without them? Why or why not?**

Read aloud 1 Corinthians 12:14-25. Then ask: **How was your team like the "body" this scripture talks about? Do you sometimes feel you're not an important part of the body? Why or why not? Think about people you know who probably don't feel they're an important part of the body. Why do they feel that way? How can you help them to feel important?**

CLOSING

Form a circle and have one kid stand in the middle. Say: **Each of you is an important part of our church body. No one should feel left out or unappreciated. So let's show each person how important he or she is by giving that person a group "squeeze."**

Have kids shout together, "You're important!" Then close around the person in the middle to give that person a big group squeeze. Do the same for each person.

 **BE MY FRIEND**

● **THEME:** Friendship
● **SCRIPTURE:** Proverbs 18:24
● **OVERVIEW:** Children learn that to have a friend they must give part of their heart away.
● **PREPARATION:** For each person, you'll need a marker, scissors, and a photocopy of the "Here's My Heart" handout (p. 83). You'll also need a Bible.

EXPERIENCE

Give children one minute to do friendly things for each other, such as waving, smiling, or patting someone on the back.

After one minute, say: **You've just done friendly things for each other. If you do these things for other people, you'll make new friends. Let's talk about what it takes to make a new friend.**

RESPONSE

Read aloud Proverbs 18:24. Ask: **What kind of friend is closer than a brother? Would you like to be that kind of friend? Why or why not?**

Give each person a marker, scissors, and photocopy of the "Here's My Heart" handout. Say: **Write the word "Friend" on your heart handout. Decorate it any way you want, then cut out the heart.**

Give kids three minutes to do this, then say: **Find a partner and give your heart to your partner. Once you have a partner's heart, cut along the dotted zigzag down the middle of the heart. Give both pieces back to your partner.**

CLOSING

Have kids hold the pieces of their hearts and close their eyes. Say: **To have a close friend, you must love that person and give away part of your heart. You don't know if the person will love you in return or if you'll ever get that piece of your heart back, but you still give it. Think of someone you'd like to be close friends with. This week give one piece of your paper heart to that person and explain what we've talked about.**

Close in prayer, thanking God for giving us close friends.

HERE'S MY HEART

Write the word "Friend" on your heart, then decorate it any way you want. Cut out the heart and give it to your partner. Wait until you are told to cut along the zigzag line.

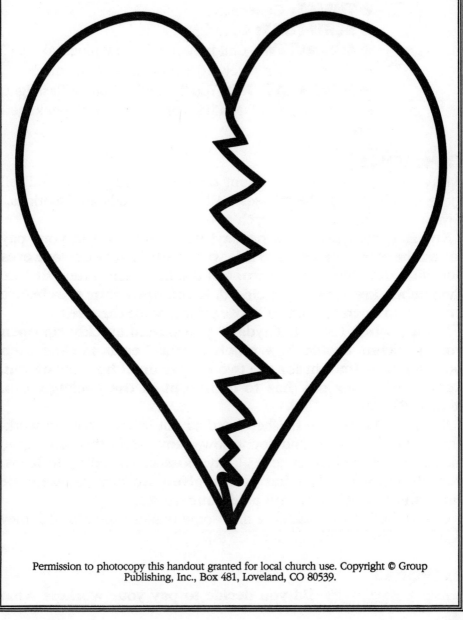

GIVE AND IT'LL BE GIVEN

● **THEME:** Generosity

● **SCRIPTURE:** Luke 6:38

● **OVERVIEW:** Children decide how much to "pay" each other, then receive the same amount themselves.

● **PREPARATION:** You'll need a Bible, a flashlight, and packages of M&M's (or some other packaged prizes).

EXPERIENCE

Have kids sit in a circle. Count off every third person and tell those people they're the "bosses." All the other kids are "workers." Give a package of M&M's to each of the bosses.

Say: **Hey, everybody, it's payday! It's time to collect your pay for all the work you've done this week! Workers, close your eyes and hold out your hand in front of the boss who's next to you. Remember, keep your eyes closed. If you open your eyes before I tell you to open them, you'll lose your pay for the week.**

Bosses, when I shout "Payday!" you should quickly rip open your package, decide how much to "pay" each worker, then pour out that amount for the two people on either side of you. Remember, your pay has to come out of the package, too. Ready? Payday!

When the bosses are finished handing out salaries, tell the workers to open their eyes and count how many M&Ms their boss gave them. Then read aloud Luke 6:38. Say: **Bosses, according to Jesus, you should get only what you've given. So pay yourself the same amount of salary you paid your workers.**

Collect the leftover M&Ms or give some bosses extra M&Ms if they don't have enough to pay themselves.

RESPONSE

Ask: **Bosses, why did you decide to pay your workers what** you did? If you'd been a worker, how would you have felt about the pay you decided on? Workers, how did you feel about your pay? If you'd been a boss instead of a worker, would you have paid your workers a different amount? Why or why not? Do you think it "pays" to be generous toward others? Why or why not? What does the Bible mean when it says, "The way you give to others is the way God will give to you"?

CLOSING

Form a circle and turn off the lights. Use a flashlight to put each person in "the spotlight" for 15 seconds. As you shine the light on each person, encourage the rest of the kids to be generous to that person by calling out what they like about him or her. After each young person has been in the spotlight, shine the flashlight all around the room for 15 seconds. Ask kids to call out what they like about God for those 15 seconds.

THE CHAIN RACE

● **THEME:** Winning

● **SCRIPTURE:** 1 Corinthians 9:24-27

● **OVERVIEW:** Children race to make paper chains and learn about competition.

● **PREPARATION:** You'll need a Bible, tape, and several 2-inch-by-8-inch construction paper slips.

EXPERIENCE

Form two teams. Give each team a pile of construction paper slips. Demonstrate how to make a circle out of construction paper, then interlock circles to make a chain. Say: **The goal of this race is for your team to make the longest chain. You have three minutes. Ready? Go!**

After three minutes, have teams stand and hold their paper chains. Determine the longest chain, then clap for the winning team.

RESPONSE

Have kids bring the chains and sit down in a circle. Ask: **What was it like to play this game? How did you feel winning? losing? When is competition good? bad?**

Say: **Competition is good when it helps get a job done or when people cooperate and work as a team. Competition is bad when it's harmful or hurts someone.**

Read aloud 1 Corinthians 9:24-27. Ask: **What does Paul say about competition? What race is Paul talking about?**

Say: **We're all winners on Jesus' team. We'll get a prize that lasts forever: We'll live with Jesus in heaven.**

CLOSING

Have kids each hold on to a part of the chain. Have each person complete the following sentence: "Dear God, in my race to be like you, help me be more..."; for example, "loving," "caring," or "willing to tell others about you."

Have kids tape the chains to the meeting room walls as reminders to keep their eyes on every Christian's goal—to serve God faithfully.

 # A PICTURE-PERFECT THANKS

● **THEME:** Honoring parents

● **SCRIPTURE:** Exodus 20:12

● **OVERVIEW:** Children make thank-you cards for their parents.

● **PREPARATION:** For each person, you'll need a sheet of construction paper, glue, scissors, crayons, a pencil, a 3×5 card, and a magazine. You'll also need a sheet of poster board and a Bible.

EXPERIENCE

Say: **Whether we have one parent or two, there are many things our parents do to make our lives special. They love us, listen to us, and give us food and clothing. What things have your parents done to make you feel special?**

Read aloud Exodus 20:12. Ask: **What does the Bible tell us about our parents?**

Say: **The Bible tells us to honor our parents—that means to make them feel special and to obey them. One way to honor parents is to thank them for the wonderful things they do for us. So, let's make thank you cards for them.**

Give each person a sheet of construction paper, scissors, glue, crayons, and a magazine. Have kids use the supplies and design thank you cards for their parents. Kids could write a big "Thank you" on their cards, then cut out and glue magazine pictures that remind them of something they're thankful for, such as a house, food, and smiles.

RESPONSE

Have each person display his or her card to the whole group, then lay it on the floor or a table to dry.

As the cards are drying, have everyone form a circle around a sheet of poster board. Ask: **Who do we thank for giving us parents?**

Write in big letters "GOD" in the center of the poster board. Give each person a 3×5 card and a pencil. Ask kids to each write on their card a prayer thanking God for all he's given them. Younger kids might want to draw pictures of things they're thankful for.

CLOSING

One at a time, have kids read their prayers of thanks or describe their pictures. Then glue the 3×5 cards to the poster board.

Pray: **Father, we thank you for giving us parents who love us and take care of us. Please help us find many ways to show them how much we love them. Amen.**

Have kids take home their thank you cards and give them to their parents.

Hang the poster board thank-you to God in your meeting room. Leave a pencil or marker close by. Each week for one month, have kids write or draw on the poster board things they're thankful for. See if you can fill the entire poster board with thanksgivings by the end of the month.

DON'T BRING ME DOWN

- ● **THEME:** Put-downs
- ● **SCRIPTURE:** Romans 12:16
- ● **OVERVIEW:** Children build a toothpick person and learn how put-downs can hurt others.
- ● **PREPARATION:** You'll need a Bible, paper, toothpicks, raisins, markers, glue, and tape.

EXPERIENCE

Form groups of no more than three or four. Give each group toothpicks, raisins, paper, and markers.

Ask each group to create a toothpick person by sticking toothpicks in raisins. The toothpick person should be able to stand on its own. Let kids eat a few raisins while they work.

After five minutes or so, tell kids to stop building their toothpick people. Ask groups to each imagine their toothpick person is someone they don't like.

Then say: **If this were really a person you didn't like, what mean things would you say to him or her? In one minute, list on your paper every mean thing you can think of—but don't list any bad words.**

After a minute, ask kids to count how many put-downs they listed. Then say: **For every mean thing you listed, remove one toothpick from your toothpick person.**

RESPONSE

Ask: **What happened to your toothpick person when you started taking away toothpicks? How did you feel as you took toothpicks away from your toothpick person? How is that like the feeling you had the last time someone said mean things to you? What really happens inside people when people say mean things to them?**

CLOSING

Read aloud Romans 12:16. Say: **Mean words don't help us get along with other people—they make us feel hurt and angry at each other. Together with your group, think of something good you can say or do for someone when you're tempted to say something mean to him or her.**

While groups are discussing, give each group some glue. Then say: **Use the toothpicks to spell out your idea on the paper you used to list your put-down ideas. You may want to break your toothpicks. Glue your spelled-out idea to the paper.** For example, kids could spell "hug," "smile," or "be nice." Supply more toothpicks if groups need them.

When groups finish, have one person from each group read their idea. Then close with a prayer asking God to help us build people up, rather than put people down.

OH SAY, CAN YOU SEE?

- ● **THEME:** Affirming others
- ● **SCRIPTURE:** Proverbs 16:24
- ● **OVERVIEW:** Children find good things in others by recognizing good things in themselves. (Best for upper-elementary kids.)

● PREPARATION: For each person, you'll need two 3×5 cards, a piece of candy, and a pencil. You'll also need a Bible.

EXPERIENCE

Tell kids they're going to look for good in other people. Then give each person two 3×5 cards and a pencil.

Say: **I changed my mind. You each have one minute to list on one card good things about yourself; for example, "nice," "friendly," and "caring." Ready? Go!**

After one minute, have kids each find a partner and read the descriptions they wrote on their card. Every 30 seconds say, "Switch partners," and have kids read their descriptions to the new partners. Switch partners at least three times.

RESPONSE

Have kids sit in a circle. Ask: **What did you think when I changed my mind and told you to write good things about yourself? Was it easy or hard to write good things about yourself? Explain. Do you think God agrees with what you wrote on your list? Why or why not?**

Say: **God made each of us good and special. He loves us. Now that we've said good things about ourselves, let's think of good things about others.**

CLOSING

Form pairs. On their second 3×5 card, have kids each write good things about their partner. When they finish writing, have partners read their good words to each other, then exchange cards.

Read aloud Proverbs 16:24. Ask: **What does this verse say about good, affirming words?**

Give each person a piece of candy to eat during the prayer. Pray: **God, let good words come from our mouths just like the good taste comes from this candy. Help our words for others be good, because of your good love for each one of us. Amen.**

Have kids keep both their cards and read the affirmations every day.

OUR HERO!

● **THEME:** Building up others
● **SCRIPTURE:** 1 John 4:7-8
● **OVERVIEW:** Children brainstorm affirmations for their "hero," then build the tallest platform for the hero to stand on. (Best for upper-elementary kids.)
● **PREPARATION:** For each person, you'll need a poster-board circle with "Hero" written on it. Attach a 16-inch piece of yarn to each circle to make a necklace. You'll also need a Bible, pencils, slips of paper, tape, and a supply of wood blocks (or wood scraps or books). Triumphant music is optional (such as the Hallelujah Chorus or the Olympics theme song).

EXPERIENCE

Form teams of no more than three or four. Have each team pick one team member to be the "hero." Give each team pencils, slips of paper, tape, and a supply of wood blocks.

Say: **Think of as many great things about your team's hero as you can, such as "good friend" and "creative." Write each good thing on a different slip of paper, then tape each slip of paper to a different block. Build a platform for your hero to stand on using only the blocks that have a "good-word" slip taped to them. The team with the tallest platform wins.**

Give kids five minutes to brainstorm and build their platforms. After five minutes, call time. Have each hero stand on his or her team's platform. Determine which team built the highest platform and lead kids in a group cheer for the winners.

RESPONSE

Ask: **How did you feel when I asked you to think of good things about your hero? Heroes, how did you feel as your team members called out good things about you? Which is harder—to think of good things about people or to think of bad things about people? Explain. How would you feel if someone treated you like a hero every day?**

Read aloud 1 John 4:7-8. Ask: **Do you agree that people who don't love one another don't really know God? Why or why not? How have you seen what God is like in this devotion? Because of Jesus, how is each one of us a hero in God's eyes?**

CLOSING

Have each person stand on a chair. Play triumphant music. Go to each child and put a hero-necklace around his or her neck. Each time, say: **You are a hero. Show God's love to others.**

COFFEE TALK

● **THEME:** Hurtful words
● **SCRIPTURE:** Psalm 19:14
● **OVERVIEW:** Children filter coffee grounds out of water and learn to filter hurtful words before they are spoken.
● **PREPARATION:** You'll need cups, water, coffee filters, coffee grounds, a spoon, a wastebasket, and a Bible.

EXPERIENCE

Say: **God wants us to be kind to one another, but sometimes we get angry and say things that hurt others. What are some things that make you angry?**

After kids tell things that make them angry, say: **Everyone gets angry sometimes, but God doesn't want us to say mean or hurtful things when we are angry. God wants all our words to be pleasing.**

Form groups of no more than three or four. Give each group a cup filled with water, an empty cup, and a coffee filter. Spoon some coffee grounds into each water-filled cup. Have one child hold the empty cup, another child hold the filter inside the empty cup, and another carefully pour the contents of the coffee-and-water-filled cup through the filter. Pass the wastebasket and have kids throw their filters and coffee grounds into it.

RESPONSE

Ask: **What happened when you poured the water and coffee grounds through the filter and into the empty cup? What did the filter do? What ended up in the empty cup? How is this like filtering out hurtful words when we talk to others? How can God help us do this?**

Say: **God has given us a filter that will help us not say mean words when we're angry. Listen to what this psalmist prayed.**

Read aloud Psalm 19:14.

Say: **When we're angry, we can ask God to make our thoughts and words pleasant and kind. God will help us sift out the hurtful words and thoughts and only say kind and good words.**

CLOSING

Have each person say, "God, I pray my words and thoughts please you." Challenge children to recite those words prayerfully the next time they're angry.

Join hands in a circle. Pray: **Lord, we know you want us to be kind to others in what we do and in what we say. Help us remember to pray to you when we feel angry so that our words and thoughts will be pleasing to you. Amen.**

RULES OF THE ROAD

- ● **THEME:** Rules
- ● **SCRIPTURE:** Joshua 1:7-8
- ● **OVERVIEW:** Children follow rules in a game and learn the value of following rules in life.
- ● **PREPARATION:** You'll need a Bible, a black marker, masking tape, and 15 sheets of construction

paper (five red and 10 green). Draw a stop sign on each red sheet and an arrow on each green sheet.

EXPERIENCE

Have kids help you clear a large area on the floor. Use the masking tape to make a huge star shape on the floor (see diagram).

Place children at different spots along the star. Say: **The object of this game is to walk along the entire star and be the first back to your starting spot. You can't run, leave the "road," (that's the masking tape) or cut corners. You can go any direction you choose and turn any time you want, but if you run into someone, you must sit down for five seconds. Ready? Go!**

After children finish, have them sit down on the star. Ask: **What happened during this game? What could we have done to make our traveling easier?**

Hold up one of the stop signs and ask: **Who knows what this sign means? What other road signs help keep our parents from getting into accidents? What would happen if we didn't have road signs or rules for driving?**

Say: **Let's hear what the Bible says about the importance of rules.**

Read Joshua 1:7-8. Ask: **What rules does God give us to live by? Why does God ask us to obey his commandments? What rules do our parents give us? Why do parents want us to follow their rules? Why is it sometimes difficult to obey God's or our parents' rules?**

Say: **Just like traffic rules, if we don't follow God's or our parents' rules, we might get into some pretty bad accidents.**

CLOSING

Place a stop sign at each intersection and an arrow sign on the side of each "point" of the star (see diagram).

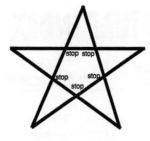

Say: **Let's play the game again. This time let's walk and obey the signs. At each stop sign, you must wait two seconds to be sure no one else is coming through. You can only travel around the points in the direction of the arrows. Let's see if we can travel around the star without any accidents.**

Traffic may still be a bit chaotic with these rules, but "accidents" should be minimal.

Have kids stop walking.

Ask: **What difference did you notice playing the game with more rules and road signs? How can we avoid "accidents" in life if we follow God's rules? our parents' rules?**

"Have the children sit down again on the star. Pray: **God, thanks for the rules you've given us to live by. Help us obey your rules and our parents' rules so that we can be safe. Amen.**

SCRIPTURE INDEX